Stopwatch

Teacher's Guide

Geraldine D. Geniusas

1

Richmond

58 St Aldates
Oxford
OX1 1ST
United Kingdom

Stopwatch Teacher's Guide Level 1

First Edition: February 2016
ISBN: 978-607-06-1250-3

© Text: Geraldine D. Geniusas
© Richmond Publishing, S.A. de C.V. 2016
Av. Río Mixcoac No. 274, Col. Acacias,
Del. Benito Juárez, C.P. 03240, México, D.F.

Publisher: Justine Piekarowicz
Editorial Team: Suzanne Guerrero, Kimberly MacCurdy,
Cara Norris
Art and Design Coordinators: Karla Avila, Jaime Angeles
Design: Jaime Angeles, Karla Avila
Layout: Erick López, Daniel Mejía, Perla Zapien
Pre-Press Coordinator: Daniel Santillán
Pre-Press Team: Susana Alcántara, Virginia Arroyo,
Daniel Santillán
Cover Design: Karla Avila
Cover Photograph: © **Thinkstock.com** Ryan McVay /
Photodisc (young man breakdancing)

Richmond publications may contain links to third party
websites or apps. We have no control over the content of these
websites or apps, which may change frequently, and we are
not responsible for the content or the way it may be used with
our materials. Teachers and students are advised to exercise
discretion when accessing the links.

The Publisher has made every effort to trace the owner of
copyright material; however, the Publisher will correct any
involuntary omission at the earliest opportunity.

Printed in Brazil by Forma Certa

Lote: 800372

Contents

Scope and Sequence

Unit	Vocabulary	Grammar	Skills
0 What's your name?	The alphabet; Numbers 0-100; Colors; Instructions; Days, months and years	Parts of speech: verbs and nouns; Subject pronouns; *Can*	**Listening:** Understanding instructions
1 What is family?	**Family Relationships:** aunt, brother, cousin, daughter, father (dad), grandfather (grandpa), grandmother (grandma), grandparent, mother (mom), nephew, niece, parent, sister, son, uncle	Demonstratives; Possessive adjectives; Possessive *'s*; Verb *be*	**Reading:** Thinking about what you know **Writing:** Making a poster **Project:** Making an infographic
2 How do you learn?	**School Places:** art room, auditorium, bathroom, cafeteria, classroom, computer lab, gymnasium (gym), laboratory (lab), library, music room **School Subjects:** chemistry, geography, math (mathematics), technology, P.E. (physical education / gym class), physics, history, science, biology	Indefinite articles; Verb *have*; Prepositions of place: *under, in, next to, on*	**Listening:** Thinking about the topic **Writing:** Making a class schedule **Project:** Making a *Perfect School* collage
3 Where are you from?	**Countries and Nationalities:** Australia / Australian, Brazil / Brazilian, China / Chinese, Egypt / Egyptian, France / French, Greece / Greek, India / Indian, Italy / Italian, Japan / Japanese, Peru / Peruvian, Thailand / Thai, The United Kingdom (The UK) / British, The United States (The US) / American, Turkey / Turkish	Verb *be*; *Can*	**Reading:** Reading in steps **Speaking:** Presenting a city or town **Project:** Making a country profile
4 What is home?	**Rooms:** bathroom, bedroom, dining room, kitchen, laundry room, living room, closet **House Objects:** bed, chair, dryer, refrigerator (fridge), shower, sink, sofa, stove, table, television (TV), toilet, washer	*There is / are; Where;* Prepositions of place: *between, in front of, on, in, next to* Short answers	**Listening:** Looking at photos and making predictions **Reading:** Reading about statistics **Project:** Designing a home

4

Unit	Vocabulary	Grammar	Skills
5 **What's your routine?**	**Routines:** brush my teeth, do homework, get dressed, go to bed, go to school, eat breakfast / lunch / dinner, take a shower, wake up **Time Expressions:** six o'clock (six a.m. / p.m.), six (oh) five, a quarter past six, half past six (six thirty), a quarter to seven	Adverbs of frequency; Present simple	**Reading:** Reading a timetable **Listening:** Thinking about questions other people will ask you **Project:** Making an agenda
6 **How important is technology to you?**	**Technology Collocations:** check e-mail, listen to music, make phone calls, make a video, play games, send messages, share photos, shop online, surf the Internet, take photos, watch movies **E-mail:** compose, delete, print, reply, save	Frequency expressions; Question words	**Reading:** Using key words **Writing:** Writing search terms for a search engine **Project:** Making a technology infographic
7 **What are you wearing?**	**Clothing:** blouse, boots, coat, dress, hat, jacket, jeans, pajamas, pants, sandals, scarf (scarves), shoes, shorts, skirt, socks, sweater, tie, T-shirt **Adjectives:** casual, cheap, comfortable, elegant, expensive, popular, useful **Prices**	Present continuous	**Listening:** Listening for detail **Writing:** Using adjectives **Project:** Making VIP profiles
8 **What do you love doing?**	**Vacation Activities:** cook, get a tan, go climbing, go shopping, go snorkeling, go surfing, go swimming, go waterskiing, lift weights, play miniature golf	Likes and dislikes; *Let's*	**Listening:** Listening for large numbers **Reading:** Identifying similarities and differences **Project:** Making a free-time-activities survey

The Concept

Stopwatch is a motivating, six-level secondary series built around the concept of visual literacy.

- *Stopwatch* constructs students' language skills from A0 to B1 of the Common European Framework of Reference (CEFR).
- A stopwatch symbolizes energy, speed, movement and competition and gives immediate feedback. The *Stopwatch* series offers dynamic, engaging activities and timed challenges that encourage students to focus and train for mastery.
- *Stopwatch* has a strong visual component to facilitate and deepen learning through authentic tasks, compelling images and the use of icons.
- The series was conceived for the international market, with a wide range of topics, incorporating cultures from around the world.

- The six-level framework of the series allows for different entry points to fit the needs of each school or group of students.
- The syllabus has been carefully structured. Each level recycles and expands on the language that was used in the previous books. This process of spiraled language development helps students internalize what they are learning.
- Each level of *Stopwatch* covers 90 – 120 hours of classroom instruction, plus an additional 20 hours of supplementary activities and materials in the Teacher's Guide and Teacher's Toolkit.

6

The Components

Stopwatch contains a mix of print and digital resources including:
- Student's Book & Workbook with Audio (print and Digital Book)
- Teacher's Guide (print and Digital Book)
- Teacher's Toolkit
- Stopwatch App (an actual stopwatch with fun vocabulary activities)

Student's Book & Workbook

Units are divided into distinct spreads, each with a clear focus:
- A **Big Question** establishes the central theme of the unit and promotes critical thinking, curiosity and interest in learning.
- **Vocabulary** is presented in thematic sets and with rich visual support to convey meaning.
- **Grammar** is introduced in context, enabling students to see the meaning, form and use of the structure.
- **Skills** (reading, listening, writing and speaking) are developed through engaging topics.
- **Culture** invites the learner to immerse oneself in the rich variety of cultures and peoples on our planet.

- **Review** activities provide consolidated practice for each of the grammar and vocabulary areas.
- In the **Project**, students apply the skills they learned in the unit to a creative task built around the Big Question.
- **Just for Fun** is a page with fun activities that teachers can assign to fast finishers.
- The **Workbook** pages offer extended practice with the vocabulary, structures and skills of the unit.
- **The Student's Audio** contains all the listening material in the units.

Teacher's Guide

Brief instructions or summaries provide a quick guide for each Student's Book activity, including **answer keys** and **audio scripts**.

A fun and engaging **warm-up** activity reviews previous knowledge and prepares students for what will be seen in each lesson.

A **wrap-up** task practices newly-learned material. Warm-ups and wrap-ups usually take the form of games.

Extension tasks promote use of language in communication and real-life situations.

Digital options provide alternatives to the projects using electronic media.

Specific questions, related to the Big Question of the unit, stimulate critical thinking.

Teaching tips help develop and enrich teachers' skills.

Teacher's Toolkit

The **Teacher's Toolkit** is a comprehensive resource that is available on the Richmond Learning Platform <https://richmondlp.com>.

- **Two optional placement tests** (beginner and intermediate) will help teachers assess their students' level of English on an individual and group basis and guide them in their choice of level and test packages.

- **Two different test packages** each contain unit tests, midterm and final exams, as well as rubrics for evaluating unit projects. There are two packages to choose from:
The *Standard* test pack for grammar and vocabulary as well as reading and listening.

The *Test Plus* test pack includes an additional communication component to assess speaking and writing. The *Test Plus* package is intended for students who are able to do all of the extension tasks in the Teacher's Guide.

- **Audio** is available in mp3 format.

- **Answer Keys** and audio transcripts for tests are included.

- **Grammar and Vocabulary Worksheets** are provided to ensure sufficient practice opportunities.

- **Reading Worksheets** (Time reading texts) are provided to offer students opportunities to develop reading skills.

- **Scorecard** forms to print or project to help students evaluate their progress are available.

Stopwatch App

The **stopwatch function** should be used for the timed activities in the Student's Book and Workbook.

Vocabulary flashcard games help students memorize words using fast-paced, fun review tasks.

The Big Question: Where are you from?

Meaningful Language in Context

8

• Teacher's Guide
- Extension activities
- Digital options for the project

• Student's Book & Workbook

• Teacher's Toolkit
- Additional readings

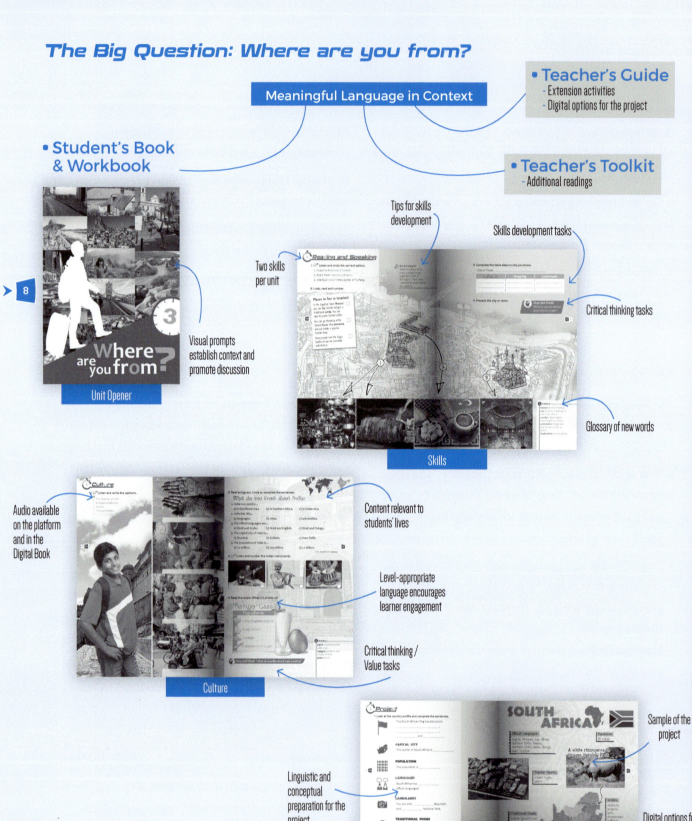

Visual prompts establish context and promote discussion

Unit Opener

Two skills per unit

Tips for skills development

Skills development tasks

Critical thinking tasks

Glossary of new words

Skills

Audio available on the platform and in the Digital Book

Content relevant to students' lives

Level-appropriate language encourages learner engagement

Critical thinking / Value tasks

Culture

Linguistic and conceptual preparation for the project

Sample of the project

Digital options for the project in the Teacher's Guide

Project

Strong Linguistic Focus

• Teacher's Guide
- Warm-ups and wrap-ups
- Teaching tips

• Student's Book & Workbook

Insight to language or content

• Teacher's Toolkit
- Exams and exam audio
- Vocabulary worksheets
- Grammar worksheets

Vocabulary

Vertical orientation of some sections to conform to visual requirements

Timed game-like activity

Grammar

Activities for fast finishers

Just for Fun

Topics expand on the unit theme

More practice with unit grammar and vocabulary

Review

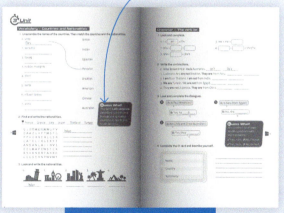

Workbook section

O What's your name?

Grammar
Parts of speech: verbs and nouns
Subject pronouns: <u>I</u> am Jo!
Can: I <u>can</u> swim.

Vocabulary
The alphabet
Numbers 0 – 100
Colors
Instructions
Days, months and years

Listening
Understanding instructions

What's your name?

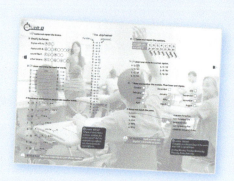

 **Teaching Tip**

Creating a Student-Centered Classroom

In order to have students be the focus of your class, use the following tips to get them involved and engaged from the beginning. Allow students to read directions for activities or examples. This prompts engagement and boosts confidence, especially for students who need extra support. Also, use your students as a resource and let them help and support each other. Finally, get to know your students, and choose content that interests them for your lessons.

Objective

Students will be able to use **letters**, **numbers**, **days** and **months** vocabulary to spell their names, say their phone numbers and say the date.

Lesson 1   Student's Book p. 8

Warm-up

Play an alphabet game.

- Write the alphabet in large letters across the board.
- Call out each letter and have students repeat. Students line up in front of the first letter of their first names.

1 **Listen and repeat the letters.**

Students repeat, following the letters in the left column and the pronunciation in the right.

2 Classify the letters.

Students write the letters that follow the same patterns.

Answers

A J K
B C D E G P T V Z
F L M N S X
H I O Q R U W Y

3 **Listen and write the number words.**

Students write out the numbers 0 to 12.

Audio Script

zero. Z-E-R-O
one. O-N-E
two. T-W-O
three. T-H-R-E-E
four. F-O-U-R
five. F-I-V-E
six. S-I-X
seven. S-E-V-E-N
eight. E-I-G-H-T
nine. N-I-N-E
ten. T-E-N
eleven. E-L-E-V-E-N
twelve. T-W-E-L-V-E

4 Pronounce the letters to decode the number words.

Students write out the numbers 13 to 20.

Answers

1. fourteen, 2. fifteen, 3. sixteen, 4. seventeen,
5. eighteen, 6. nineteen, 7. twenty

5 Think Fast! Spell your name and say your phone number.

Students do a one-minute timed challenge: they spell their names and say their phone numbers.

- Draw students' attention to the **Guess What!** box. Read the information aloud and ask students to raise their hands if there is a zero in their phone numbers. Remind them to pronounce it as *oh*.

Wrap-up

Review the alphabet using objects.

- Hold up some simple classroom objects and elicit their names, e.g., *pencils, pens, books, rulers*, etc.
- Students spell the name of the object. Write the letters on the board as the student says them.

➠ (No homework today.)

🐾 Teaching Tip

Guiding Pair Work Activities Effectively
There are many benefits to using pair work in the classroom: pair work takes the focus off you and puts it on the learners, it gives students more speaking time, it raises their confidence and changes the pace of the lesson. However, avoid losing control of the class—set a signal to start and to finish—and having each student work at a different pace. Finally, if it gets noisy, make sure students stay on task and can hear each other.

Unit 0

Warm-up

Practice or teach the following rhyme:

- *Thirty days has September, April, June and November. All the rest have thirty-one, except for February alone. It has 28 days every year, 29 in a leap year.*

- Explain that there are 365 days in a year, except for leap years. A leap year happens every four years and has 366 days, with one extra day in February.

6 🎧 ⁰³ **Listen and repeat the numbers.**

Students repeat the numbers they hear.

Audio Script

thirteen, thirty
fourteen, forty
fifteen, fifty
sixteen, sixty
seventeen, seventy
eighteen, eighty
nineteen, ninety

7 🎧 ⁰⁴ **Listen and circle the correct option.**

Students circle the numbers they hear.

Answers

1. 14, 2. 15, 3. 60, 4. 70, 5. 18, 6. 90

Audio Script

0. *thirty*
1. fourteen
2. fifteen
3. sixty
4. seventy
5. eighteen
6. ninety

8 🎧 ⁰⁵ **Read and number the months. Then listen and repeat.**

Students put the months in order and then repeat the months they hear.

Answers

October 10, *February* 2, *June* 6, *April* 4, *December* 12, *January* 1, *May* 5, *March* 3, *July* 7, *September* 9, *November* 11, *August* 8

Audio Script

January, February, March, April, May, June, July, August, September, October, November, December

9 **Read and match the years.**

Students match years with the way they are said.

Answers

1. nineteen forty-five, 2. twenty sixteen,
3. nineteen oh (zero) three, 4. twenty twenty-five

10 **Think Fast! Spell months and days for a classmate to guess.**

Students do a two-minute timed challenge: they spell out the months and days.

- Draw students' attention to the *Guess What!* box. Read the information aloud and ask students if this is true in their language.

Wrap-up

Review numbers, months and years.

- Review numbers by writing numbers in numeral form on the board and ask students to spell them out.

- Review months by writing two months with a blank between them on the board, e.g., *April _____ June*. Ask students which month is between April and June.

- Review years by writing years in numeral form on the board and asking students to say them aloud. If necessary, remind students that we usually say the first two numbers as one number and then the second two numbers as one number.

- You can also use a calendar to review.

▐▐▐➡ **(No homework today.)**

Objectives

Students will be able to understand instructions they hear. They will be able to identify **colors**. They will also be able to identify basic **verbs and nouns** used in the classroom, identify the correct **subject pronouns** and understand the **modal** *can* for ability.

Lesson 3   Student's Book p. 10

Warm-up

Play a game of *Simon Says*.

- Elicit or provide verbs your students know, e.g., *stand up, sit down, open your books.* Mime the actions as you say them.

- Ask students to stand up, using the phrase *Simon says.* Say *Simon says, Stand up!* Students should all stand up. Explain that you must say the phrase *Simon says* before the command. If you don't, the students shouldn't act it out.

- After one or two actions, don't use the phrase; say only *Open your books!* Any student who performs the action must sit down.

- Play as long as time permits or until there is only one student left standing.

11 🎧 06 Listen and match the parts of the sentences.

Students match verbs with the appropriate phrases to make imperative sentences.

Audio Script

0. Listen to the conversation.
1. Look at the board.
2. Write your name.
3. Circle the correct option.
4. Read the text.
5. Open to page 21.

12 Look and circle the correct option.

Students identify vocabulary by circling the correct words that name the pictures.

Answers

1. page 21, 2. name

13 Read and circle the words.

Students identify which words are nouns and which are verbs.

Answers

1. *nouns* dictionary, person, Paula, Oliver, July, Monday, computer
2. *verbs* talk, listen, write, look, read

14 Look at the words and say the colors.

Students identify the colors of particular words.

Answers

dictionary gray, *English* purple, *talk* red, *person* green, *Paula* yellow, *Oliver* black, *listen* brown, *July* purple, *write* white, *Monday* gray, *look* green, *computer* brown, *read* red

15 Read and complete the patterns.

Students practice days of the week, numbers and months vocabulary by completing patterns.

Answers

1. fifteen, 2. thirteen, 3. October, 4. eight, 5. ninety

Wrap-up

Review commands.

- Remind students of the icons and corresponding words in Activity 11, miming the actions: for *listen,* hold your hand up to your ear.

- Play *Simon Says,* as done in the Warm-up, using the commands from the unit.

- Have volunteer students come to the class and "play" Simon.

➠ **(No homework today.)**

Unit 0

Warm-up

Review the concepts of singular and plural.

- Play a game called *Salt and Pepper*. Students go around the room, alternately saying *Salt* and *Pepper*. Explain that the students who said *Salt* represent singular nouns; the students who said *Pepper* represent plural nouns.

- Use objects in your classroom, e.g., a book, pencils, erasers, etc. Hold up one object, e.g., a book, to illustrate *singular*. The Salt students should stand up. Then show more than one object, e.g., a handful of pencils. The Pepper students should stand up.

- Play as long as time permits and students are engaged.

14

16 Look and write the correct subject pronoun.

Students identify and write the correct subject pronouns.

- Direct students to the **Subject Pronouns** chart.

- Ask *What color is the pronoun for the girl?* Elicit *blue*. Then ask *What color is the pronoun for the boy?* Elicit *green*. Point out the colors of the names in the activity.

- Have students compare answers in pairs.

Answers

1. They, 2. He, 3. She, 4. We, 5. They, 6. It

17 Classify the subject pronouns.

Students identify whether subject pronouns are singular or plural.

Answers

singular I, she, he, it
plural we, they

18 Read and mark (✓) the sentences that are true for you.

Students indicate what they can do.

- Draw students' attention to the **Can** box and read the information aloud.

- Mimic and say a few examples, using recently learned verbs, e.g., *I can listen. I can write. I can read.*

Answers

Answers will vary.

19 Think Fast! Read and complete the sentences.

Students do a one-minute timed challenge: they share some personal favorites.

- Have students complete the exercise. Then encourage them to share their information with their classmates in either a whole-class setting or in small groups.

Answers

Answers will vary.

Extension

- Play a game called Truth or Lie? Make two different lists of at least five verb phrases from the unit and others your students know. Begin the list like this:

- *Can you … ride a bike / speak English / eat ten chocolate bars?*

- Model the activity first. Have a student ask you the questions. Answer all of them honestly, using *Yes, I can* or *No, I can't*, except for <u>one</u> question. Your answer to this question should be a lie. Students guess which of your answers is the lie.

- Students ask and answer questions in small groups of three or four.

? Big Question

Students do a mingle activity.

- Remind them of the Big Question, *What's your name?* Ask what other questions they can ask. Remind them of what they've learned over the past two lessons. Elicit or provide questions:
  - » *What month were you born?*
  - » *What year were you born?*
  - » *What are some of your favorite things, like your favorite colors, days of the week or months?*
  - » *What can and can't you do?*

Elicit answers: *I'm twelve. October. 2004.* Write the questions and answers on the board.

- Explain that you are going to play some music, and when the music is playing, students walk around the room. When the music stops, they stop and talk to the person nearest to them, asking and answering questions.

➡ **(No homework today.)**

1 What is family?

Grammar	Vocabulary
Demonstratives: <u>This</u> is my cat. **Possessive adjectives:** Owen is <u>my</u> brother. **Possessive 's:** My brother<u>'s</u> name is Owen. **Verb *be*:** Sara and Maggie <u>are</u> sisters. <u>Is</u> Alicia your aunt?	**Family Relationships:** aunt, brother, cousin, daughter, father (dad), grandfather (grandpa), grandmother (grandma), grandparent, mother (mom), nephew, niece, parent, sister, son, uncle

Reading	Writing
Thinking about what you know	Making a poster

What is family?

In the first lesson, read the unit title aloud and have students look carefully at the unit cover. Encourage them to think about the message in the picture. At the end of the unit, students will discuss the big question: *What is family?*

🗩 Teaching Tip

Keeping a Vocabulary Notebook

Throughout this course, students will encounter vocabulary sets. These words are grouped by theme: family relationships, school places, etc. It is easier for students to remember words in this way. In order to make the most of this presentation format, have students keep a notebook for vocabulary. Encourage them to add mind maps, diagrams, translations and examples—anything that will make the target language more memorable. They can also use their vocabulary notebooks for review.

 **Vocabulary**

Objective

Students will be able to use **family relationships** vocabulary to talk about their families.

Lesson 1   Student's Book pp. 14 and 15

Warm-up

Students discuss the question *What is family?*

- Draw students' attention to the illustration on page 13.
- In pairs, have students discuss how the pictures on each box answer the question *What is family?*
- Ask each pair to share one or two of their explanations with the class.

1 🎧 ^{07} **Listen and complete the family tree using the words in the box.**

Students listen to Lee describe his family and label the photos on his family tree with the correct family relationships vocabulary.

Answers

Carol grandmother, *Joey* grandfather, *Roy* father, *Alexis* mother, *Kirsty* aunt, *Thomas* uncle, *Janice* sister, *Scott* brother, *Gary* cousin

Audio Script

Hi. I'm Lee, and this is my family. Roy is my father. Alexis is my mother. Janice is my sister. Scott is my brother. Joey is my grandfather. Carol is my grandmother. Gary is my cousin. Kirsty is my aunt. Thomas is my uncle.

2 **Read and identify the person.**

Students read the clues and use the family tree to identify the person. They write the name on the line.

Answers

1. Lee, 2. Gary, 3. Gary, 4. Kirsty

Extension

Students make their first entries in their vocabulary notebooks.

- Elicit different ways to provide meaning for new vocabulary: *use a picture, a translation, an example, a mind map, a definition, write the word with its opposite.*
- Ask students to say which way works well for family relationships vocabulary.
- Students make family relationships entries in their vocabulary notebooks.

Wrap-up

Review family relationships vocabulary using a family tree.

- Make your own family tree and bring it to class. Alternatively, use the family tree on page 14.
- Point to different family members and elicit the relationship. Say, *This is my …* Let students complete the sentence.
- Challenge students to talk about your family tree using: *This is your mother / grandfather / cousin.*

➡ **Workbook p. 126, Activities 1 and 2**

Lesson 2   Student's Book p. 15

✔ Homework Check!

Workbook p. 126, Activities 1 and 2

Answers

1 Look and write the name.

1. Chris, 2. Beth, Veronica, 3. Jason, Chris

2 Decode the new words.

1. niece, 2. uncle, 3. daughter, 4. nephew

Warm-up

Students practice family relationships vocabulary.

• Write *son, daughter, niece, nephew* on the board. Elicit the gender (male / boy, or female / girl) for each word.

• Use the family tree on page 14. Present these sentences for students to identify the person:

  1. Alexis is my daughter.

  2. Janice is my niece. Kirsty is my sister.

  3. Scott is my nephew.

  4. Alexis is my sister. Gary is my son.

Answers

1. Carol or Joey, 2. Thomas, 3. Thomas or Kirsty, 4. Kirsty

---

3 **Imagine you are a member of this family. Write clues for a classmate to guess the person.**

Students write sentences that are true for a person in the family tree. They write two sentences for each item. They can use Activity 2 as a model.

4 **Think Fast! Read a classmate's clues and guess the person.**

Students do a one-minute timed challenge: they form pairs or small groups and exchange books. They read their classmates' clues and identify the family members.

5 **Classify the family words in the chart.**

Students categorize family relationships words by gender.

• Draw students' attention to the **Guess What!** box. Read the information aloud and ask students to identify Lee's family members using the new words.

Answers

Male: father (dad), grandfather (grandpa), brother, uncle, son, nephew

Female: mother (mom), grandmother (grandma), sister, aunt, daughter, niece

Both: cousin, parents, grandparents

Extension

Students make a simple family tree in their notebooks and present it to a classmate.

• Give students five minutes to draw their own family trees.

• Form pairs. Have students describe their family trees to each other: *(Anna) is my mother.*

• If necessary, students can write the sentences and read them to their partner.

• Monitor and offer help as needed. Make note of any mistakes and give anonymous feedback after the activity.

• Students can form new pairs for more practice.

Wrap-up

Practice spelling.

• Say family relationships words for students to spell aloud or write.

• Have students continue the challenge in pairs or small groups.

▸ **Workbook p. 126, Activities 3 and 4**

Teaching Tip

Teaching Additional Vocabulary

Students often ask for additional vocabulary: *How do you say [stepfather]?* That's good! They're engaged in the topic and they need a word to express a meaning that is important to them. Encourage students to write the word down in their vocabulary notebooks in case they need it later. However, avoid teaching too many extra words or phrases. Students may struggle to remember the target vocabulary in addition to a long list of unfamiliar words.

⏱ Grammar

Objective
Students will be able to use **demonstratives, possessive adjectives, possessive 's** and **the verb be** to talk about families.

Lesson 3   Student's Book p. 16

✔ **Homework Check!**

Workbook p. 126, Activities 3 and 4

Answers

3 Write the word.

1. dad, 2. parents, 3. grandma, 4. grandpa,
5. grandparents

4 Find and write eight family words.

```
G R A N D M A L E L R A U N T E H N D Q
S O N I I U Y V G A O N N V L S J I A Z
W F K T Z Q A P P O K U C R O J S E D B
M S T X H C T L A L E F L D A P G C L F
D A U G H T E R Q W B N E I W B W E T X
F M W B Q Y W I G C O U S I N P L T V D
```

grandma, aunt, son, uncle, niece, dad,
daughter, cousin

Warm-up

Students do a one-minute timed challenge: they complete male-female word pairs to review family relationships vocabulary.

• Write the following word pairs on the board to complete:

1. brother and _____

2. aunt and _____

3. mom and _____

4. grandma and _____

5. son and _____

6. niece and _____

Answers

1. sister, 2. uncle, 3. dad, 4. grandpa, 5. daughter,
6. nephew

1 Look, read and complete the sentences.

Students learn and practice *this, that, these* and *those* by completing sentences with the correct demonstratives.

• Direct students' attention to the **Demonstratives** box. Read the information aloud and ask students to find each word (*this, that, these, those*) in the picture above.

Answers

1. These, 2. This, 3. Those, 4. This, 5. That

2 🎧 08 Listen and repeat the words.

Students practice pronouncing *this, that, these* and *those*.

• Make sure students place their tongue between their teeth to pronounce the voiced *th* sound, which can be difficult for students to produce.

Audio Script

this, this
these, these
that, that
those, those

3 🎧 09 Listen and memorize the rhyme.

Students recite and memorize the rhyme to help them remember the forms of the demonstratives.

Audio Script

This, that, these and those,
This is the way the T-H goes.
If you see your tongue pop out,
Then you have it all worked out!

Wrap-up

Review the demonstratives using objects in the classroom.

• Hold or point to an object (or multiple objects) in the classroom. It is not necessary to say the name of the object.

• Elicit the corresponding demonstrative.

 Workbook p. 127, Activities 1 and 2

💬 Teaching Tip
Modeling the Activity
Activity instructions can be hard for students to understand, especially beginners. Use simple wording, and whenever possible, do the first item or two together as a class as a model. Then students can imitate the procedure for the rest of the activity. In this way, you can avoid confusion and misunderstandings and ensure that the activity is effective.

Warm-up

Play a game to review demonstratives.

- Pass out thirteen pieces of paper (or fewer if there are fewer students). Have each student with a piece of paper write one family relationship word on it in large letters. Say each word aloud and have a student write it on his or her paper: *aunt, brother, cousin, dad, daughter, grandma, grandpa, mom, nephew, niece, sister, son, uncle.*

- Stand in the center of the room and have the students holding a piece of paper with a family relationship word on it move around the room, with some standing near you and some standing farther away. Have the students holding *mom* and *dad* and *grandma* and *grandpa* stand together.

- Divide the remaining students into two groups. Explain to students that you will point to your "family members" and the groups will compete to say the correct sentence using demonstratives first.

- Model the activity by pointing to a "family member" and saying the sentence yourself: *That is my brother.*

- Have students switch roles, move around the room and play the game again.

◀ **Underline the possessive adjectives and complete the chart.**

Students identify and underline possessive adjectives. Then they complete the table with the possessive adjectives they underlined.

- Remind students to look at the photos. They clarify the meaning of the sentences.

Answers

1. My, his, 2. Their, 3. My, her

From top to bottom: my, his, her, their

5 Read and complete using *is* or *are*.

Students determine when to use the singular and plural forms of *be*.

Answers

1. is, 2. are, 3. are, 4. is

6 Think Fast! **Look and write the sentences.**

Students do a five-minute timed challenge: they use the visual prompts to form sentences with demonstratives, possessive adjectives and the verb *be*.

Answers

1. These are my grandparents. 2. Their names are Paul and Shirley. 3. That is my father. 4. His name is Bill.

Wrap-up

Students use their family trees to identify family relationships.

- Form pairs. Have students identify their family relationships to each other: *This is my mother.*

- Encourage them to ask about names: *What's her name? Her name is (Anna).*

- Students can form new pairs for more practice.

▐▐▶ **Workbook pp. 127 and 128, Activities 3–7**

Preparing for the Next Lesson

Ask students to watch a video about elephant calves at a California zoo: goo.gl/z0mw2W.

Reading & Writing

Objectives

Students will be able to think about what they know. They will also be able to make a poster.

Lesson 5 — Student's Book pp. 18 and 19

✔ **Homework Check!**

Workbook pp. 127 and 128, Activities 3–7

Answers

3 Complete the chart.

I, my, *you*, your, *he*, his, *she*, her, *it*, its, *we*, our, *they*, their

4 Replace the phrase with a possessive adjective.

1. His name is Bob. 2. Their names are Leo and Matt. 3. Her name is Leonora.

5 Complete the sentences.

1. My, 2. His, 3. Their, 4. your

6 Look and write the sentences.

1. Nathan is my brother. 2. Simon and Alex are my cousins. 3. That is my cat. 4. These are my parents.

7 Complete the questions in Activity 6.

1. Is Nathan, 2. Are Simon and Alex, 3. Is that, 4. Are these

Warm-up

Students play a guessing game to preview the reading.

- Tell students you are going to tell them some facts about elephants; one will be false. They should guess which.
  - » *Elephants can swim.*
  - » *Elephants eat 90 – 275 kilograms of plants in a day.*
  - » *Elephants drink around 50 liters of water every day.* (False: They drink 100 – 200 liters!)
  - » *Elephants are the largest land animal in the world.*

- Take a vote to find out which fact students think is false.

1 Look at the pictures. What do you know about elephant families?

Students look at the illustrations of a text to activate prior knowledge.

- Draw students' attention to the **Be Strategic!** box. Read the information aloud and ask students how this strategy can help them understand a text.

2 Read and circle T (True) or F (False).

Students read for comprehension and identify true and false statements.

Answers

1. T, 2. F (Cousins are in the herd.), 3. F (The grandmother is the leader.), 4. T

Wrap-up

Students review what they have read.

- Check comprehension of the text.

- Provide several slips of paper for each student. Give students one minute to write down as many things about the text as they can remember on individual slips of paper. Encourage them to keep their books closed.

- Collect the papers in a bag. Pull out each one and read it aloud, or have a more confident student read them. Students say if the fact is correct.

➡ **Workbook p. 129, Activity 1**

Teaching Tip

Managing Fast Finishers

Some students complete activities more quickly than others, so it's a good idea to have a few extra activities on hand, otherwise these students may become bored and disruptive. One set of activities designed for fast finishers are the **Just for Fun** pages. Students can work on these individually and then check their answers in the back of the Student's Book. The **Just for Fun** activities for this unit are on page 26.

> ✔ **Homework Check!**
>
> Workbook p. 129, Activity 1
>
> **Answers**
>
> **1 Look at the pictures and circle the correct answer.**
>
> 1. b, 2. a

Warm-up

Students predict the meaning of icons.

- Show students the icons on page 19 without letting them see the headings. Ask them to say what they think they mean.
- Students open their books to check.

3 Look and complete the sentences.

Students read facts about elephants and use the facts to complete sentences.

Answers

1. Africa and Asia, 2. many types of plants, 3. 70, 4 to 7 tons

4 Choose one elephant fact and draw a mini poster.

Students expand on a fact by making a poster to illustrate it.

Stop and Think! Critical Thinking

Is it OK to have circus elephants?

- Ask students *What is a circus?*, and *What do elephants do in a circus?*
- Point to the elephants in the photo on pages 18 and 19 and ask *How do you think life is different for elephants in the wild and circus elephants?*
- Building on the previous discussion, ask *Is it OK to have circus elephants?*
- Have students discuss in groups or discuss as a class.

Wrap-up

Review what students have learned.

- Play a game of Jeopardy! to review the elephant facts.
- Students form two to three teams. Draw a grid on the board similar to this one:

Family	Diet	Live	Size
10	10	10	10
20	20	20	20
30	30	30	30

- Students take turns asking for questions: *Family for 20.* Read the question and allow the team members to discuss the answer. The student whose turn it is answers. If he answers correctly, his team gets the number of corresponding points. Cross out the number if answered correctly. If answered incorrectly, the next team may ask for that question.

- Continue with the other teams until all questions have been answered or as time permits.
- The team with the most points in the end wins. Some questions you can use (with answers in parentheses) are:

Family	Diet	Live	Size
What is a group of elephants called? (a herd)	What do elephants eat? (many types of plants)	What region do elephants live in? (Africa and Asia)	What is the largest land animal in the world? (the elephant)
How many members live in a group? (12)	How much food do elephants eat every day? (90 – 275 kg)	What is their habitat? (forests and grasslands)	How much does a baby elephant weigh? (100 kg)
Who is the leader of the group? (a female, the grandmother)	How much water do elephants drink every day? (100 – 200 liters)	How long do elephants live? (70 years in the wild)	How much does an adult elephant weigh? (4–7 tons)

➡ **Workbook p. 129, Activities 2 and 3**

 *Culture*

Objectives
Students will be able to explore Australian English and talk about enjoying time with family.

Lesson 7 Student's Book pp. 20 and 21

> ✔ **Homework Check!**
> Workbook p. 129, Activities 2 and 3
>
> **Answers**
> **2 Read and complete the notes.**
> *Weight* 25 to 50 kg, *Diet* fruit and plants (80%) and meat (20%), *Longevity* up to 50 years.
> **3 Read and circle the correct animal.**
> the dolphin

Warm-up
Engage students in the topic.
- Hold up the picture on page 20 for students to see.
  - » Point to the Christmas tree and ask *What time of year is it?*
  - » Point to the beach and ocean and ask *Where are they?*
  - » Point to the people's swimsuits and ask *What are they wearing?*
  - » Point to the barbeque, the people with the surfboard and the sandcastle and ask *What are they doing?*
  - » Point to the map, focusing on Australia, and ask *What country is this?*

1 Read the sentences and circle the correct option.
Students guess some facts about Australia.

Answers
1. southern, 2. New Zealand, 3. Aborigines, 4. koalas, 5. Canberra

2 Read the comic and circle to complete the sentences.
Students read a comic and learn some Australian expressions and traditions. The complete the sentences with the correct options.

Answers
1. c, 2. a, 3. a, 4. b

Wrap-up
Students practice discovering meaning from context.
- Have students underline all of the words in the comic that Emily is confused about.
- Form pairs and tell students to imagine that they are Emily. Have them look closely at the pictures in the comic.
- Challenge students to find clues in the context of the situation that Emily could have used to discover the meaning of the Australian words.
- Invite students to share the clues they discovered with the class.
- Some possible answers are: *Togs: Everyone except Emily is wearing a swimsuit. Barbies: When her cousin asks if she has barbies, the family members are holding barbecued meats. Esky: Emily could see what Chris got the food out of. Ace: Chris looks happy with Emily's answer. Tucker: The adults have been cooking and are inviting the kids to come eat.*

➠ (No homework today.)

Warm-up

Confirm comprehension of a text by
asking questions.

- Ask students some questions to help them recall
  the reading: 1. *Where is the family?* 2. *What holiday is
  it?* 3. *Who's visiting?* 4. *What's funny about the comic?*

Answers

1. In Sydney, Australia, at the beach, 2. Christmas,
3. Emily, their cousin from Vancouver, Canada.
4. Emily speaks English, but she can't understand
everything her family says.

3 Write the Australian English words.

Students identify the Australian English words in the
comic and label the photos with the correct words.

Answers

1. prawns, 2. togs, 3. esky, 4. barbie, 5. tucker

Stop and Think! Value

What activities do you do with your family?

- Ask, *What activities does Emily's family in Australia do?*
  Elicit *They barbeque food and surf.*

- Ask *What activities do you do with your family?* Ask
  *Are there special activities you and your family do on
  holidays?* Students form small groups to discuss.

- Monitor, offering help as needed. Don't focus
  on accuracy. Allow students to express and share
  their thoughts.

Extension

Students learn expressions from other English-
speaking cultures.

- Give students some English words from other
  English-speaking countries and have them guess
  the meaning. Some examples of British English:
  fancy (like), *fortnight* (two weeks), *kip* (sleep),
  wonky (not right), *cooker* (stove), *tad* (a little
  bit), *queue* (line of people). Some examples of
  Canadian English: *biffy* (toilet), *chesterfield* (sofa),
  eh? (you know?), *runners* (running shoes). Some
  examples of Irish English: *bang on* (exactly), *black*
  (crowded), *cacks,* (pants), *cat* (no good), *dear*
  (expensive), *gaff* (apartment), *donkey's years* (a
  long time).
- Alternatively, challenge students to do some
  research and find out some words on their own.

Wrap-up

Students review Australian English and other
English words.

- Students form pairs and write a short dialogue
  using Australian English or another culture's
  English words.

- Students practice the dialogue in pairs.

- Challenge students by having them switch their
  dialogues with another pair. Then the pair has to
  "translate" the other's dialogue.

▌▌▶ **(No homework today.)**

Project

Objective
Students will be able to make an infographic.

Lesson 9   Student's Book pp. 22 and 23

Warm-up
Students identify the parts of a mind map.

- Have students study the mind map. Ask them to say what they think goes into the ovals.

- Elicit or provide *headings*.

1 Look at the Woods Family infographic on page 23. Write the headings from the infographic in the mind map.
Students use information from an infographic to complete a mind map.

Answers

left to right, top to bottom Favorite Foods, Fun Activities, The Woods Family, Quick Facts

2 In your notebook, make a mind map about your family.
Students use the model of a mind map from Activity 1 to make one about their own families.

> **The Digital Touch**
> To incorporate digital media in the project, suggest one or more of the following:
> - Go online to make a digital mind map: https://www.mindmup.com/
> - Create your mind map in software like Word or Google Docs.
> Note that students should have the option to do a task on paper or digitally.

Wrap-up
Students review and share their mind maps.

- Give students an opportunity to look over their mind maps. Write these questions on the board to help them self-edit their work: *Are the headings correct? Are all my family members here? Is there any missing information about my family? Is the spelling correct?*

- Ask students to think about what is included on the mind map. Ask *Are there any other categories or boxes you would add?*

- Encourage students to edit their mind maps at home if time runs short.

Warm-up

Review mind maps.

- Students look at their mind maps to prepare them for making an infographic about their families.

- Students can compare their mind maps with the one on page 22 and with other students'. Encourage them to make any final touches.

3 Make a pie chart for your infographic.
Students make a pie chart about their families' activities.

4 Make an infographic about your family. Present it to the class.
Students finish the infographic about their families and present it to the class.

The Digital Touch

To incorporate digital media in the project, suggest one or more of the following:

- Prepare your infographic on a computer. Upload pictures of your family and use icons and different fonts. You can use a Word program or software like Google Docs.
- Create your pie chart online: goo.gl/PKbV9j.
- Put the information about your family in PowerPoint slides and present your infographic to the class.

Note that students should have the option to do a task on paper or digitally.

Wrap-up

Students compare their infographics.

- Students form small groups and share the infographics about their families.

- Encourage students to find out whether their families have any activities in common. Tell students to compare the amounts of time their families spend on different activities and note the similarities and differences.

- Have groups summarize the results of their comparisons for the class.

➡ **Workbook p. 128, Activities 1 and 2 (Review)**

⏱ Review

Objective

Students will be able to consolidate their understanding of the vocabulary and grammar learned in the unit.

Lesson 11 · Student's Book p. 24

> ✔ **Homework Check!**
>
> Workbook p. 128, Activities 1 and 2 (Review)
>
> **Answers**
> **1 Read and correct the sentences.**
> 1. ~~brother~~ Those are my brothers, Tyson and Chad. 2. ~~Our~~ My name is Peter. 3. ~~sister name's~~ My sister's name is Renee. 4. ~~Hugo is~~ Is Hugo your uncle? 5. ~~Is~~ Are they your brothers?
> **2 Complete the table.**
> *grandfather*, *grandmother*, grandpa, *grandma*, *parent*, parent, uncle, *aunt*, *son*, daughter, cousin, *cousin*, *brother*, sister, father, *mother*, *dad*, mom, nephew, *niece*

Warm-up

Students list the vocabulary and grammar they have learned in the unit.

- Ask students to think of what they've learned in this unit.
- Elicit and list the grammar and vocabulary on the board. Vocabulary: family relationships *(father [dad], mother [mom], parents, brother, sister, uncle, aunt, grandmother [grandma], grandfather [grandpa], grandparents, cousin)*. Grammar: demonstratives *(this, that, these, those)*; possessive adjectives *(my, your, her, his, its, our, their)*; the verb *be (is, are)*.

1 Look and complete the sentences.
Students complete a passage based on a family tree.

Answers
1. grandparents, 2. father, 3. mother, 4. cousin, 5. uncle, 6. aunt

2 Read and circle *T* (True) or *F* (False).
Students identify true and false statements based on a family tree.

Answers
1. F (Michael is William's brother. William doesn't have a sister.), 2. T, 3. F (Michael is Lisa's uncle.), 4. F (Lisa is Gavin's cousin.)

3 Look and complete using *this, that, these* or *those*.
Students complete sentences using the correct demonstrative pronouns.

Answers
1. Those, 2. This, 3. These, 4. That, 5. These, 6. That

Wrap-up

Students use their family trees to talk about their families.

- Have students take out their family trees.
- Model with a student by pointing to someone on her family tree and asking *Who's this?* Elicit an answer: *This is my sister.* Then ask *What's her name?* Elicit an answer.
- Students form pairs and talk about their families. Don't worry if students don't ask *Who's this?* as long as they are talking about their family members. Encourage them to use the grammar and vocabulary from the unit.

➡ **(No homework today.)**

Lesson 12 Student's Book p. 25

Warm-up

Remind students of what they reviewed in the previous lesson.

- Ask students what they've reviewed so far. Elicit *family relationships* and *demonstratives*.

- Ask students to say what they will be reviewing today. Elicit *possessive adjectives* and *the verb* be.

4 Follow and write the possessive adjectives.

Students write the possessive adjectives that correspond to each personal pronoun.

Answers

from top to bottom your, their, his, my, its, our, her

5 Look and circle the correct option.

Students identify the correct possessive adjectives based on pictures.

Answers

1. their, 2. his, 3. his, 4. our

6 Write questions using *is* and *are*.

Students use cues to write questions using *is* and *are*.

Answers

1. Is Jackie his aunt? 2. Are Ryan and Katie your cousins? 3. Is that his sister? 4. Are those our neighbors? 5. Is Ellen her grandmother? 6. Are these my parents?

❓ Big Question

Students are given the opportunity to revisit the Big Question and reflect on it.

- Tell students to turn to the unit opener on page 13 and think about their own families.

- Have students take out their family trees and the infographic they made about their families and look them over.

- Students form small groups to discuss the following questions:
  » *How much time do you spend with your family? Is it enough? Would you like to spend more?*
  » *What kinds of things do you with your family? What's your favorite thing to do with them?*
  » *Do you have any pets? Are they part of your family? Why or why not?*

- Monitor closely as your students discuss their thoughts. Don't focus on accuracy. Just allow students to express themselves, and encourage them to use the target language correctly.

Scorecard

Hand out or project a *Scorecard*. Have students fill in their *Scorecards* for this unit.

▸ **Study for the unit test.**

Grammar

Indefinite articles: <u>a</u> lamp, <u>an</u> eraser, <u>a</u> university, <u>an</u> mp3 player

Verb *have*: He <u>has</u> a telephone. / They <u>have</u> notebooks. / Do you <u>have</u> a pencil?

Prepositions of place: *under, in, next to, on*: <u>in</u> the box, <u>on</u> the box, <u>next to</u> the box, <u>under</u> the box

Vocabulary

School Places: art room, auditorium, bathroom, cafeteria, classroom, computer lab, gymnasium (gym), laboratory (lab), library, music room

School Subjects: chemistry, geography, math (mathematics), technology, P.E. (physical education/gym class), physics, history, science, biology

Listening

Thinking about the topic

Writing

Making a class schedule

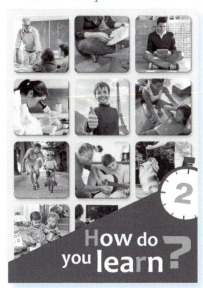

How do you learn?

In the first lesson, read the unit title aloud and have students look carefully at the unit cover. Encourage them to think about the message in the picture. At the end of the unit, students will discuss the big question: *How do you learn?*

🗨 Teaching Tip

Giving Feedback and Correcting Mistakes

Feedback is important for student learning, but it can difficult for any of us to accept criticism. Consider giving anonymous feedback after an activity. When students are engaged in a free-speaking activity, make note of any serious errors and mistakes you hear, especially mistakes in the target language. After the activity, write some of the more common mistakes on the board. Then have the students correct the mistakes as a class, in pairs or in small groups. This approach helps students develop fluency when speaking, and it also boosts their confidence when they know they can correct their own mistakes.

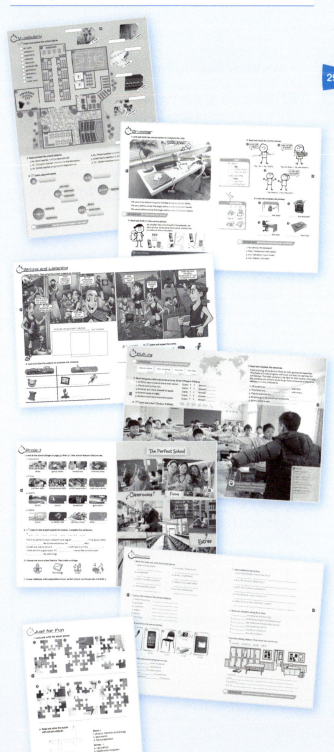

 **Vocabulary**

Objective

Students will be able to use **school places** and **school subjects** vocabulary to talk about their school.

Lesson 1   Student's Book pp. 28 and 29

Warm-up

Students do a timed challenge: they brainstorm school places and schools subjects.

• Divide the class into small groups.
• Tell them they have one minute to write the names of school places.
• Then give them one minute to brainstorm and write the names of schools subjects.
• As a whole class, students share their lists.

1 ¹⁰ **Listen and number the school places.**

Students practice school places vocabulary while they listen for the pronunciation.

Answers

art room 8, *auditorium* 10, *bathrooms* 5, *cafeteria* 9, *classroom* 3, *computer lab* 4, *gymnasium* 2, *laboratory* 1, *library* 7, *music room* 6

Audio Script

SCHOOL PRINCIPAL: Welcome to Lakeview Middle School. Here is a map of our facilities.
1. This is the laboratory.
2. This is the gymnasium.
3. This is a classroom.
4. This is the computer lab.
5. These are the bathrooms.
6. This is the music room.
7. This is the library.
8. This is the art room.
9. This is the cafeteria.
10. This is the auditorium.

2 **Read and label the school subjects.**

Students match school subjects with their corresponding school places.

Answers

From top to bottom geography, chemistry, math, physics, P.E., technology

Extension

• Have students make a map of your school, similar to the one on page 28.
• Form pairs and have them compare their maps.

Wrap-up

Students practice school places and school subjects vocabulary in context.

• Have students form pairs and take turns saying sentences about the school places and school subjects. For example, *Ms. Sanders teaches art in classroom 4B.*

• If students did the Extension activity, have them use their maps.

• Monitor, offering help as needed. Make note of any mistakes and have an anonymous feedback session after the activity.

➠ **Workbook p. 130, Activities 1 and 2**

✔ **Homework Check!**

Workbook p. 130, Activities 1 and 2

Answers

1 Look and write the school subjects.
0. art 1. music, 2. chemistry, 3. mathematics
2 Write the short forms of the words.
1. lab, 2. math, 3. gym

Warm-up

Students play a guessing game to review school places and school subjects vocabulary.

- Say some information about a school place and subject at your school. For example, *I teach math in classroom 1A.* Ask students to guess the teacher.

- Have them take turns asking about school places and subjects and guessing the teachers.

3 🎧" Listen, clap and repeat.

Students identify the stressed syllables in the vocabulary words.

- Draw students' attention to the smaller circles within the larger circles. Have students read the words connected to the larger circles silently.

- Ask students what they think the smaller circles represent. Elicit or provide: *The circles represent the syllables, the large circles represent the stressed syllables.*

Audio Script

[1 loud clap] math
[1 loud clap, 1 small clap] art room, classroom, bathroom, physics
[2 equal claps] P.E.
[1 loud clap, 2 small claps] library, music room, chemistry
[1 loud clap, 3 small claps] laboratory
[1 small clap, 1 loud clap, 2 small claps] computer lab, gymnasium, geography, technology

---

4 Think Fast! Add the school subjects to the chart.

Students do a five-minute timed challenge (use your Stopwatch app to time it): they complete a chart with school subjects and school places.

- Draw students' attention to the *Guess What!* box. Read the information aloud and point out the highlighted words, asking students to locate the subjects on the map in Activity 1.

Answers

From left to right, top to bottom math, P.E., geography, technology, physics, chemistry

---

Wrap-up

Students practice word stress in the vocabulary.

- Draw students' attention to the chart. Model with a student, clapping and saying a word in the chart. Encourage the student to do the same.

- Have students form pairs and take turns clapping and saying the words in the chart.

▶ **Workbook p. 130, Activity 3**

Grammar

Objective

Students will be able to use **indefinite articles, the verb** *have* **and prepositions** to talk about school subjects and objects.

Lesson 3   Student's Book p. 30

✔ **Homework Check!**

Workbook p. 130, Activity 3

Answers

3 Classify the school words.

School Subjects geography, physics, science, biology, math, chemistry

School Places laboratory, music room, cafeteria, classroom, library, auditorium

---

Warm-up

Play a game to practice singular and plural nouns.

• Say the names of different objects in the classroom. For example, *door, lamps, desks, book.*

• Have students raise one arm if the object is singular and both arms if the object is plural.

1 Look and circle the correct option to complete the rules.

Students learn rules about indefinite articles.

Answers

singular, consonant, vowel

2 Think Fast! **List five words that use** *an.*

Students do a one-minute timed challenge: they think of and write five words that use *an.*

• Draw students' attention to the **Guess What!** box. Read the information aloud and ask students to think of other examples.

3 Read and mark (✓) the correct picture.

Students identify the picture that corresponds to the text.

Answer

the third picture

Wrap-up

Students play Pictionary to review indefinite articles.

• Have a student come to the front of the class. Whisper the name of an object and ask him or her to draw it on the board.

• Set a stopwatch. Encourage the rest of the class to guess the name of the object before the time runs out: *an eraser, a tablet, pencils.*

• Have students take turns drawing the objects.

• Continue playing as a whole class at the board or in small groups until you have used all the vocabulary words from the unit.

➠ **Workbook p. 131, Activity 1**

> ✔ **Homework Check!**
>
> Workbook p. 131, Activity 1
>
> **Answers**
>
> **1 Number the objects in alphabetical order.
> Then write *a* or *an*.**
>
> 11 a *stapler*, 2 an *encyclopedia*, 9 a *pen*, 5 a *marker*, 6
> a *notebook*, 10 a *pencil*, 12 a *USB drive*, 1 a *calculator*,
> 8 a *paper clip*, 3 an *envelope*, 7 a *paintbrush*, 4 an
> *eraser*

Warm-up

Review school objects vocabulary.

- Write the names of objects in the classroom on
  small pieces of paper.

- Place the labels on the wrong objects. For example,
  put the label *desk* on a chair.

- Set a stopwatch. Students race against the clock to
  put the correct labels on the objects.

- If you have a big class, make multiple copies of the
  labels so each student can participate.

4 Read and circle the correct answer.

Students practice questions and short answers
with *have*.

- Draw students' attention to the ***Have*** box. Make a
  few sentences with *have*, referring to the pictures,
  e.g., *I have a pencil. She has an eraser. They don't have
  a dictionary.* Challenge students to make the first
  two sentences negative (*I don't have a pencil. She
  doesn't have an eraser.*) Challenge them to make the
  last sentence affirmative. (*They have a dictionary.*)

Answers

1. Yes, I do. 2. Yes, she does. 3. No, they don't.

5 Look and complete the phrases.

Students practice prepositions of place.

- Draw students' attention to the ***Prepositions*** box.
  Say, *Look at the cat. Where is it?* Provide the first
  answer: *The cat is in the box.* Point to the second
  picture and ask again, *Where is the cat?* Elicit: *The cat
  is on the box.* Continue with the last two pictures:
  The cat is next to the box. The cat is under the box.

Answers

1. under, 2. in, 3. next to, 4. on

6 Think Fast! Write the questions.

Students do a one-minute timed challenge: they
write questions using *have* and prepositions.

Answers

1. Does he have a phone in his backpack? 2. Do
they have notebooks on their desks? 3. Do you
have a calculator in your locker? 4. Does she have a
stapler on her desk?

Wrap-up

Review questions using *have*.

- Lay out some items on your desk, e.g., pencils,
  pens, note cards, books, etc. Ask questions: *Do
  I have a book?* Elicit the answer. Assign different
  objects to different students randomly.

- Have students form groups and ask and answer
  questions about what they have. Monitor, offering
  help as needed.

▶ Workbook pp. 131 and 132, Activities 2–6

Preparing for the Next Lesson

Ask students to watch an introduction to Ancient
Greece from Study.com: goo.gl/rr3lnO or invite them
to look around on the BBC website: goo.gl/xazbHV.

Writing & Listening

Objectives

Students will be able to think about the topic. They will also be able to make a class schedule.

Lesson 5   Student's Book pp. 32 and 33

✔ **Homework Check!**

Workbook pp. 131 and 132, Activities 2–6

Answers

2 Write the subjects under the correct verb forms.

have / don't have Chris and Pete, Tim and I, You

has / doesn't have Lisa, Paul, The teacher

3 Read the schedule and complete the sentences.

1. doesn't have, 2. have, 3. has, 4. doesn't have, 5. has

4 Write the questions.

1. Does Bailey have biology in the morning?

2. Does she have technology in the afternoon?

3. Does Bailey have music this year?

5 Complete the chart.

No, I don't. *Yes, he* does. *No, he* doesn't. *No, you* don't. *Yes, they* do.

6 Look and complete the sentences.

1. next to, 2. on, 3. under, 4. in, 5. next to

Warm-up

Review school subjects and school places vocabulary.

- If students made a map of their school in the Extension activity in Lesson 1, have them take it out. If not, draw their attention to the map on page 29.

- Students form groups and take turns saying sentences about the school. For example, *Coach Harris teaches P.E. in the gymnasium.* Monitor, offering help as needed.

1 Read the comic. Then write the school subjects to compare.

Students complete a Venn diagram to compare Ancient Greece's school subjects to their own.

Answers

School in Ancient Greece music, literature, mathematics, science, P.E., *My School* Answers will vary. *Both* Answers will vary.

2 Look and label the subjects to complete the schedule.

Students identify icons that correspond to school subjects.

Answers

In the Morning music, literature, *In the Afternoon* math, P.E., science

Wrap-up

Students summarize a story.

- Draw students' attention to the comic again. Ask them to reread it.

- Students form groups and take turns telling each other about Lukos's school schedule. Monitor, offering help as needed.

➠ **Workbook p. 133, Activity 1**

 Teaching Tip

Managing Fast Finishers

Some students complete activities more quickly than others, so it's a good idea to have a few extra activities on hand, otherwise these students may become bored and disruptive. One set of activities designed for fast finishers are the *Just for Fun* pages. Students can work on these individually and then check their answers in the back of the Student's Book. The *Just for Fun* activities for this unit are on page 40.

> ✔ **Homework Check!**
>
> Workbook p. 133, Activity 1
>
> **Answers**
>
> **1 Read and number from 1 to 4 (1 = most important, 4 = least important).**
> Answers will vary.

Warm-up

Students think about the topic before they listen.

- Draw students' attention to the **Be Strategic!** box. Read the information aloud and ask students to tell you what the topic was of the reading in the previous lesson. Elicit *School subjects in Ancient Greece.*

- Draw students' attention to the pictures and labels in Activity 3. Read the words aloud or have a student read them.

- To check comprehension, mime the actions and ask students to say the word.

3 🎧¹² **Listen and repeat the words.**
Students hear and repeat vocabulary words.

Audio Script
baking, sewing, dance, cooking, childcare, weaving

4 🎧¹³ **Listen and number the subjects.**
Students listen to a monologue and number the subjects in the order they hear them.

Answers

baking 3, *sewing* 2, *dancing* 1, *cooking* 5, *childcare* 6, *weaving* 4

Audio Script
Hello, I'm Damaris. My brother goes to school, but I don't. I work and learn at home with my mother. In the morning, I learn dancing with a teacher. I also learn sewing and baking from my mother. In the afternoon, I learn weaving and cooking. Finally, I learn childcare—I take care of my little sister.

5 **Design icons and make a schedule for your classes.**
Students use the schedule on page 32 as a model for making their own schedules.

Stop and Think! Critical Thinking

Should schools teach subjects like cooking, sewing and dance? Should they teach childcare? Why? Why not?

- Write *PROS* and *CONS* on the board. Ask students what they think these terms mean (positive and negative).

- Students form small groups of three or four and make lists of the pros and cons of learning the school subjects listed.

- When students have finished, have a member from each group go to another group to share their groups' ideas and thoughts.

- Don't focus on accuracy here. Allow students to speak freely.

Wrap-up

Students talk about their school schedules.

- Have students take out the schedules they made in Activity 5.

- Students form pairs and use school subjects vocabulary to talk about their schedules.

- Encourage students to use school places vocabulary to tell each other where they have their classes as well.

➡ **Workbook p. 133, Activities 2 and 3**

 **Culture**

 36

Objectives

Students will be able to learn about school in China. They will also be able to think about how their time is spent.

Lesson 7 — Student's Book pp. 34 and 35

> ✔ **Homework Check!**
>
> Workbook p. 133, Activities 2 and 3
>
> **Answers**
>
> **2 Read and complete the chart.**
> *Homeschooling* parents are teachers, study at home, *Traditional Schools* professional teachers, study at school, *Both* school subjects, exams, go to museums
>
> **3 Imagine that you study at home. In your notebook, make a schedule for your school day.**
> Answers will vary.

Warm-up

Students discuss how they spend their time at school.

- Draw emoticons or faces on the board and label them: *no free time* (angry face), *some free time* (neutral face), *lots of free time* (happy face).

- Ask students to think about how they spend their time on school days. As a class, discuss whether or not students feel they have enough free time.

1 Think Fast! Complete the table about your school day.
Students do a one-minute timed challenge: they fill in a table with the number of hours they spend on different activities during their school day.

Answers

Answers will vary.

2 Read and guess which sentences are true. Circle T (True) or F (False).
Students guess whether statements about school in China are true or false to generate interest in the listening.

Answers

Answers will vary.

3 🎧 **14 Listen and write T (True) or F (False).**
Students listen to check their guesses.

Answers

1. T, 2. F (Classes start at 7 or 7:30.), 3. F (Students have a long break for lunch.), 4. T, 5. T

Audio Script

School is very important in China. Even in middle school, students often live at their school. In the morning, they start classes at 7 or 7:30. They have a long break for lunch. Then they have more classes. In the afternoon, they have a break for exercise. Classes end at 6:00 p.m., but students study at night, too. Students study because they have many important exams.

Wrap-up

Students discuss their thoughts on the listening.

- Ask students if any of the information in the listening surprised them.

- Initiate further discussion by asking some of the following questions: *Would you like to live at your school? What are some pros (positive things) about a long school day? What are some cons (negative things)? How important are exams at school? Has your opinion about how much free time you have changed?*

➡ **(No homework today.)**

Lesson 8 Student's Book pp. 34 and 35

Warm-up

Students predict information about a text to generate interest.

- Draw students' attention to the photo on pages 34 and 35.

- Ask, *What do you see in the photo? Where are they? Who is in front of the class? Do you do exercise at school?* Ask students to share their thoughts.

◀ Read and complete the sentences.

Students read a text and complete sentences to practice reading comprehension.

Answers

1. radio gymnastics, 2. radio program,
3. ten minutes, 4. professional athletes,
5. competitive

Stop and Think! Value

What are the advantages and disadvantages of intense studying?

- Remind students of the Wrap-up activity for the previous lesson. Ask them to summarize their discussions.

- Then ask students to think about the pros (advantages) and cons (disadvantages) of intense studying, like students do in China. Students form pairs to make lists.

- Students form small groups to discuss the question.

- Challenge students to debate the question: half the class is for intense studying, the other half is against it.

- When students are ready, have one person from each group come to the front of the class to present their argument for or against intense studying.

- Be sure to give feedback after the debate.

Wrap-up

Students discuss their thoughts on what they've learned.

- Ask students to say what they've learned about schools in China.

- Initiate further discussion by asking some of the following questions:

  » *The reading states that exercise "helps students to be alert for their studies." Is exercise important for learning?*

  » *Is being competitive in schools good?*

- You may wish to have students discuss these questions in small groups.

 (No homework today.)

Teaching Tip
Using Group Work

Group work gives students the chance to practice the language they've acquired. Here are some tips for using group work:
Encourage students to speak fluently. Don't worry about accuracy too much, except for the target language. Allow students to support each other. Be thoughtful about the groups you form: you may want to have students of similar ability working together, or you may want to have mixed-ability groups. Be sure to let students move around: just getting them up and in a different seat in the classroom can help expend some of that extra energy! And, when appropriate, wrap up group work activities by having one student from each group report to the class.

Project

Wrap-up

Students revisit their thoughts about their own school after hearing about one student's idea of a perfect school.

- Go back to the list on the board of things students like about their school.

- Ask students to compare what they like about their school with the features of the perfect school described in the listening and on the collage.

- Ask students which of the features of the perfect school in the listening they like or do not like.

▶ **(No homework today.)**

Lesson 9   Student's Book pp. 36 and 37

Warm-up

Students discuss what's good about their school.

- Ask students to brainstorm what's good about their school. Write their ideas on the board.

- Students form small groups and discuss what's good about their school. Encourage them to say why and explain their opinions. Monitor, offering help as needed.

- Challenge students to discuss what's *not* so good about their school.

 38

1 **Look at the school collage on page 37. Mark (✓) the school features that you see.**

Students identify features of a school presented in a collage.

Answers

1. desks, workshops, group tables, 2. math and science, 3. tennis, 4. a pool, other: a library

2 🎧¹⁵ **Listen to the student explain his choices. Complete the sentences.**

Students listen to a student talk about his perfect school and complete the sentences with words from the audio.

Answers

desks, would, practical, important, future, fun, really

Audio Script

This is my perfect school. It doesn't have regular desks. It has group tables. I would like to have workshops for practical skills. A math and science focus is important. It will help me in the future. I think tennis is a good sport. It's fun. I would like to have a pool. I really like swimming!

Warm-up

Students think of other school features.

- Students form small groups of three or four. They brainstorm other school features.

- Come together as a class and write some of the features on the board. Some features students may think of include clubs (drama, chess, robotics, Lego, math, English, etc.), after-school activities, peer mentoring, field trips, a school newspaper. Supply new vocabulary as needed.

3 Choose one more school feature. Then make a collage.

Students make a collage of school features.

- You will need poster board, magazines and other pictures, scissors, glue and markers for this project. Students may work on the project in small groups.

- Draw students' attention to the school features pictured. Additionally, draw their attention to the list on the board from the Warm-up.

- Students choose at least one more school feature and make a collage of their perfect school, either from pictures or drawings. Draw their attention to the features in Activity 1 and to the collage on page 37 to use as a model.

4 In your notebook, write a description of your perfect school. Use the phrases in Activity 2.

Students write a paragraph based on a model and their collages.

> **The Digital Touch**
>
> To incorporate digital media in the project, suggest one or more of the following:
> - Make your collage online: goo.gl/onuzf, or goo.gl/eEU4u.
>
> Note that students should have the option to do a task on paper or digitally.

Wrap-up

Students share their collages.

- Students present the information in their collages, based on the description of their perfect schools.

- When students have finished their presentations, display the collages in the classroom.

 Workbook p. 132, Activities 1 and 2 (Review)

39

 **Review**

Objective

Students will be able to consolidate their understanding of the vocabulary and grammar learned in the unit.

 Lesson 11 Student's Book p. 38

> ✔ **Homework Check!**
>
> Workbook p. 132, Activities 1 and 2 (Review)
>
> **Answers**
> **1 Read and circle the correct option.**
> 1. a, 2. a, 3. a, 4. an, 5. an
> **2 Look and rewrite the sentences.**
> 1. Lilly and Sophie don't have karate after school.
> 2. I don't have physics with Ms. Jones. 3. Does Matt have lunch in the cafeteria?

Warm-up

Students list the vocabulary and grammar they have learned in the unit.

- Ask students to think of what they've learned in this unit.

- Elicit and list the grammar and vocabulary on the board. Vocabulary: school subjects (*chemistry, English, geography, math, music, P.E., physics, science, technology*); school places (*art room, auditorium, bathrooms, cafeteria, classroom, computer lab, gymnasium, laboratory, library, music room*). Grammar: indefinite articles (*a, an, these, those*); the verb *have* (*have, has, don't / doesn't have*); prepositions of place (*in, on, next to, under*).

1 **Read the clues and write the school places.**
Students identify school places vocabulary from clues.

Answers

1. art room, 2. gymnasium, 3. auditorium, 4. library, 5. music room, 6. classroom, 7. cafeteria, 8. laboratory

2 **Correct the names of the school subjects.**
Students correct the spelling of school subjects.

Answers

1. physical education, 2. geography, 3. chemistry, 4. English, 5. science, 6. technology

3 **Look and circle the correct option.**
Students identify the correct indefinite article.

Answers

1. a, 2. a, 3. a, 4. an, 5. an, 6. a

4 **Complete the sentences using *have* or *has*.**
Students review the use of the verb *have*.

Answers

1. have, 2. has, 3. have, 4. has, 5. have

Wrap-up

Students talk about what their classrooms have.

- Ask students to think about what features your classrooms at school have. If necessary, elicit a few features: *group tables / desks, computers, a smart board*.

- Have students form pairs to discuss. Monitor, offering help as needed.

➡ **(No homework today.)**

Warm-up

Remind students of what they reviewed in the previous lesson.

- Ask students to say what they've reviewed. Elicit *School places, school subjects, articles and affirmative sentences with* have.

- Ask students to say what they will be reviewing today. Elicit *Questions and negative sentences with* have *and prepositions of place.*

5 Unscramble the sentences.

Students put words in the correct order to make sentences.

Answers

1. Mike has a tablet in his locker. 2. Do you have a dictionary? 3. My parents don't have a TV. 4. Does Amanda have a phone? 5. My sister doesn't have a calculator.

6 Read and complete using *Do* or *Does*.

Students use the correct auxiliary verb with *have*.

Answers

1. Do, 2. Does, 3. Does, 4. Does, 5. Do, 6. Does

7 Find the missing objects. Then write four sentences.

Students review the use of prepositions of place.

Answers

1. The pencil is under the book. 2. The jacket is in the locker. 3. The backpack is next to the desk. 4. The calculator is on the desk.

8 Think Fast! Describe the locations of five objects in your classroom.

Students do a two-minute timed challenge: they use objects in the classroom to practice prepositions of place.

? Big Question

Students are given the opportunity to revisit the Big Question and reflect on it.

- Tell students to turn to the unit opener on page 27 and think about the discussion they had in the Warm-up in Lesson 1: How do you learn vocabulary?

- Students form small groups and discuss the question "How do you learn?" Remind students of the reading about students in Ancient Greece and the school in China. Remind them about the features of their perfect school.

- Monitor as students discuss the Big Question, offering help as needed.

- Come together as a class. Ask students if their viewpoints on learning have changed, and if so, how.

★ Scorecard

Hand out (and/or project) a *Scorecard*. Have students fill in their *Scorecards* for this unit.

▥▶ **Study for the unit test.**

3 Where are you from?

Grammar	Vocabulary
Verb *be*: They <u>are</u> omnivores. ***Can*:** Polar bears <u>can</u> swim.	**Countries and Nationalities:** Australia / Australian, Brazil / Brazilian, China / Chinese, Egypt / Egyptian, France / French, Greece / Greek, India / Indian, Italy / Italian, Japan / Japanese, Peru / Peruvian, Thailand / Thai, The United Kingdom (The UK) / British, The United States (The US) / American, Turkey / Turkish

Reading	Speaking
Reading in steps	Presenting a city or town

Where are you from?

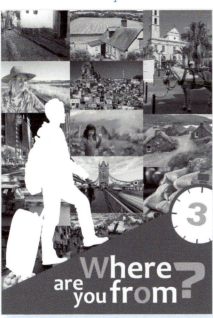

In the first lesson, read the unit title aloud and have students look carefully at the unit cover. Encourage them to think about the message in the picture. At the end of the unit, students will discuss the big question: *Where are you from?*

43

Teaching Tip

Focusing on Fluency vs. Accuracy

Focusing on accuracy helps students produce grammatically correct written and spoken English. However, being concerned with accuracy sometimes means sacrificing fluency. Fluency increases as learners progress and become more comfortable using English. Students become more comfortable speaking and writing in English when they are given the opportunity for fluency. Consider when accuracy is the right approach (a controlled grammar or vocabulary activity, for example) and when fluency is appropriate (a communicative or free-writing activity).

Vocabulary

Objective

Students will be able to use **countries and nationalities** vocabulary to talk about geography and where people are from.

Lesson 1 Student's Book pp. 42 and 43

Warm-up

Students discuss where they're from.

- Students turn to page 54 in their Student's Book. Draw students' attention to the world map. Ask them to locate their country.

- Model by saying *I'm from [country]. Where are you from?* Elicit or provide *I'm from [country]*.

- Students brainstorm what they know about their country, for example, what the capital is, what the flag looks like, what the national animal is, what some important landmarks are.

1 🎧¹⁶ Listen and number the landmarks.

Students are exposed to countries as they number landmarks.

Answers

1, 3, 7, 6, 5, 8, 4, 2

Audio Script

1. The Sydney Opera House is in Australia.
2. Christ the Redeemer is in Brazil.
3. The Great Wall of China is in China.
4. The Great Pyramid is in Egypt.
5. The Taj Mahal is in India.
6. Machu Picchu is in Peru.
7. The Tower Bridge is in the United Kingdom.
8. Central Park is in the United States.

2 🎧¹⁷ Listen and write the nationality for each country.

Students practice nationalities while they listen for spelling.

- Draw students' attention to the **Guess What!** box. Read the information aloud.

Answers

1. Australian, 2. Brazilian, 3. Chinese, 4. Egyptian, 5. Indian, 6. Peruvian, 7. British, 8. American

Audio Script

1. The Sydney Opera House is an Australian landmark. A-U-S-T-R-A-L-I-A-N.
2. Christ the Redeemer is a Brazilian landmark. B-R-A-Z-I-L-I-A-N.
3. The Great Wall of China is a Chinese landmark. C-H-I-N-E-S-E.
4. The Great Pyramid is an Egyptian landmark. E-G-Y-P-T-I-A-N.
5. The Taj Mahal is an Indian landmark. I-N-D-I-A-N.
6. Machu Picchu is a Peruvian landmark. P-E-R-U-V-I-A-N.
7. The Tower Bridge is a British landmark. B-R-I-T-I-S-H.
8. Central Park is an American landmark. A-M-E-R-I-C-A-N.

Extension

Students play a guessing game about countries.

- Make sets of cards, or have your students make them, with names of countries on them.

- Model the activity by choosing one of the cards, not letting students see. Say a sentence to give students a clue about the country, for example, *I'm walking on the Great Wall. Where am I?* Elicit *You're in China.*

- Students form pairs. Give each pair a set of cards. Students take turns making statements, giving clues to each other to guess the countries.

Wrap-up

Students review countries and nationalities vocabulary.

- Have students turn to page 54 in their Student's Book and look at the world map.

- Ask students to find the countries from the lesson on the map.

- Challenge them to remember the landmarks and say sentences using the nationalities.

➠ **Workbook p. 134, Activity 1**

✔ **Homework Check!**

Workbook p. 134, Activity 1

Answers

1 Unscramble the names of the countries. Then match the countries and the nationalities.

1. Australia, Australian, 2. Egypt, Egyptian,
3. United Kingdom, British, 4. India, Indian,
5. Brazil, Brazilian, 6. United States, American,
7. China, Chinese

Warm-up

Students play a word game with countries and nationalities vocabulary.

- Write the names of countries they learned in Activity 2 on the board, with just the first letter and then dashes for the other missing letters, e.g., A _ _ _ _ _ _ _ _ (Australia).

- Have students form pairs. Tell them to take turns guessing the country names and corresponding nationalities.

3 Read and match.

Students match nationalities with the corresponding countries.

Answers

1. France, 2. Turkey, 3. Italy, 4. Thailand, 5. Greece,
6. Japan

4 Classify the nationality words.

Students identify and categorize patterns of nationality words.

Answers

Country + -ian or -n American, Australian, Brazilian, Egyptian, Indian, Italian, Peruvian
Country + -ish British, Turkish
Country + -ese Chinese, Japanese
Other Thai, French, Greek

5 Think Fast! **In your notebook, write eight nationality words in alphabetical order.**

Students do a five-minute timed challenge: they write nationality words in alphabetical order.

Answers

American, Australian, Brazilian, British, Chinese, Egyptian, French, Greek, Indian, Italian, Japanese, Peruvian, Thai, Turkish

Extension

Students play a game of Bingo to practice countries and nationalities.

- On a piece of paper, have the students draw a grid, like this:

- Have students write a country name in each box.
- Write all the nationality names on pieces of paper. Put the pieces in a box or bag.
- Choose one piece of paper and read the nationality word aloud and set the paper aside. Students cross out the corresponding country name.
- Continue reading aloud other nationality words.
- Name the first student who crosses out all their country names correctly and shouts *Bingo!* the winner.

Wrap-up

Students review nationalities.

- Open the Student's Book to page 43, showing the national flags for the six countries studied in Activity 3. Tell students to cover the names with a piece of paper so that only the flags are visible.

- Have students form pairs. Ask them to take turns pointing to the flags and having their partners say the country and nationality words.

➠ **Workbook p. 134, Activities 2 and 3**

Grammar

Objective

Students will be able to use **the verb** *be* and **the modal** *can* to talk animals and their abilities.

Lesson 3   Student's Book pp. 44 and 45

✔ Homework Check!

Workbook p. 134, Activities 2 and 3

Answers

2 Find and write the nationalities.

Italian, Japanese, Thai, Turkish, French, Greek

3 Look and write the nationalities.

1. British, 2. American, 3. Brazilian, 4. Egyptian

Warm-up

Students brainstorm animals they know in their own country.

• Have students form groups of three or four. Ask them to make a list of animals that live in their own country.

• After a few minutes, have the groups share their lists with the whole class.

• Ask students to share their experiences. Here are some questions to generate discussion: *What animal is [color]? What animal is [small / big]? Which are your favorites?*

1 Read and label the information cards.

Students learn facts about some endangered species.

• Draw students' attention to the photos. Ask them if they know where any of the animals live.

• Read the title of the reading aloud: Endangered Species. Ask students if they know what that means. Explain that when a species is endangered there are very few of that species left in the wild, or nature.

• Draw their attention to the glossary. Go over the words and their glosses before reading.

Extension

Students are exposed to animals from the countries they've learned.

• Draw students' attention to the countries and nationalities on page 43.

• Ask *Can you think of animals that live in these countries?*

• Have students form groups of three of four. Set a stopwatch for three minutes and have them brainstorm animals they know. Provide new vocabulary words as necessary.

• Have the groups share their lists with the rest of the class.

Wrap-up

Students discuss their reactions to the text.

• Ask students to discuss the information in the texts. Here are some questions: *Did they learn something new? Did any of the information surprise them? Do they know of any organizations that are trying to help these animals?*

➠ **Workbook p. 135, Activities 1–3**

Lesson 4   Student's Book pp. 44 and 45

> ✔ **Homework Check!**
>
> Workbook p. 135, Activities 1–3
>
> **Answers**
> **1. Look and complete.**
> 1. are = you're, 2. is, 3. we're, 4. they + are
> **2. Write the contractions.**
> 1. aren't, They're, 2. I'm, I'm not, 3. We're, aren't,
> 4. aren't, They're
> **3. Look and complete the dialogues.**
> 1. isn't, 2. are

Warm-up

Students are exposed to the verb *be* with some facts about endangered animals.

- Write the following animals on the board: *orangutan, giant panda, Siberian tiger, polar bear.*

- Tell students that each country goes with one animal.

- Write these prompts on the board: *1. _____ are from Russia. 2. The _____ is from China. 3. _____ are from Canada. 4. This _____ is from Indonesia.*

- Have students guess which animal corresponds to each country and write the appropriate sentences. Explain that they will fill in the blank with the singular or plural of the animal depending on the form of the verb *be* used in the sentence. Invite students to read their answers aloud.

Answers

1. Siberian tigers, 2. giant panda, 3. Polar bears,
4. orangutan

2 **Underline the forms of *be* in the information cards.**
Students identify forms of *be* in texts.

Answers

They are carnivores., They're the biggest cats in the word., They are carnivores., Their fur isn't white. It's clear!, They are omnivores., They are omnivores., They aren't white. They're gray!, They are omnivores.

3 **Think Fast!** **Look and write the contraction.**
Students do a one-minute timed challenge: they write the contractions of the verb *be.*
- Draw students' attention to the *Guess What!* box. Read the information aloud.

Answers

1. aren't, 2. they're, 3. it's, 4. isn't, 5. aren't, 6. I'm,
7. you're, 8, she's, 9. he's, 10. we're

4 **Complete the information card with the correct form of the verb *be.***
Students practice writing the correct form of *be.*

Answers

are, are, re

Wrap-up

Students practice the verb *be* by playing a game.

- Have students form groups of five or six to play a guessing game. Make sets of cards of six animals each and put them in as many bags.

- Give each group a bag of cards. Have one student in each group draw a card from the bag and describe the animal to the other members in the group for them to guess.

- Repeat this steps until every student has drawn a card.

➠ **Workbook pp. 135 and 136, Activities 4 and 5**

Teaching Tip

Giving Different Types of Feedback

Giving constructive criticism and praise helps students maintain a positive attitude toward their learning. Feedback can take various forms. Verbal feedback can be as simple as saying, *That's right!* or *Nice work!* or repeating the mistake a student made to encourage self-correction. Visual feedback can be expressions or gestures such as a thumbs-up or a nod of the head. When a student makes a mistake, some forms of visual feedback include a look of confusion or a shake of the head. Be consistent so students can pick up on that quickly. Finally, written feedback is most useful on homework, exams, quizzes and writing assignments. This is a great opportunity to not only focus on what areas students still need to work on, but on what they did well.

# Reading & Speaking

Objectives

Students will be able to read in steps. They will also be able to present a city or town.

Lesson 5   Student's Book pp. 46 and 47

✔ **Homework Check!**

Workbook pp. 135 and 136, Activities 4 and 5

Answers

4 Complete the ID card and describe yourself.
Answers will vary.
5 Write sentences using *can* or *can't*.
1. Tortoises can't jump 3 meters in the air. 2. Polar bears can swim 50 kilometers. 3. Tigers can run 60 km per hour. 4. Pandas can't run 60 km per hour.

Warm-up

Students say what they know about a country.
- Hold up the Student's Book on page 46. Show students the pictures and ask them to guess the country. Give them a hint: *It's one of the countries from Lesson 1.*
- Ask students what they know about Turkey. *What's the capital? What language do people speak there?*, etc.
- Brainstorm and elicit answers from the whole class.

1 18 Listen and circle the correct option.

Students listen to a boy speaking about the country he is from.

Answer

1. Turkish, 2. Istanbul, 3. isn't

Audio Script

Hi. I'm Fusun Ozil. I'm from Istanbul and I'm Turkish. Istanbul is a very important city in Turkey, but it isn't the capital. The capital of Turkey is Ankara.

2 Look, read and number.

Students read a text and identify corresponding photos.
- Draw students' attention to the *Be Strategic!* box and read the information aloud. Make sure students understand the concepts of *a general idea* and *details*.

Answers

2, 1, 3

Wrap-up

Students discuss their reactions to a text.
- Have students summarize what they learned about Turkey. If helpful, write these questions on the board: *What is the capital of Turkey? What kind of food can you have in Istanbul? Where can you buy souvenirs in Istanbul? Why do people visit the Hagia Sophia?* Students form pairs and discuss what they've learned. Encourage them to share their thoughts and opinions.

➡ **Workbook p. 137, Activity 1**

🗨 Teaching Tip

Managing Fast Finishers

Some students complete activities more quickly than others, so it's a good idea to have a few extra activities on hand, otherwise these students may become bored and disruptive. One set of activities designed for fast finishers are the *Just for Fun* pages. Students can work on these individually and then check their answers in the back of the Student's Book. The *Just for Fun* activities for this unit are on page 54.

✔ **Homework Check!**

Workbook p. 137, Activities 1 and 2

Answers

1 Read and mark (✓). What can you see in Patara?

wildlife, water slides, ruins

2 Read again and circle *T* (True) or *F* (False).

1. T, 2. F (Tourists can visit Roman ruins and see wildlife.), 3. T, 4. F (Patara is a good destination for families.)

Warm-up

Students talk about their own city or town.

- Draw students' attention to the text in Activity 2. Have them read the text again.
- Have students form groups of three and talk about their own city or town using the information in the text.

3 Complete the table about a city you know.

Students personalize the topic by filling in the table with information about landmarks, shopping and local foods in a city they are familiar with.

Answers

Answers will vary.

4 Present the city or town.

Students share information about the city or town they wrote about in Activity 3 by presenting their information to the class.

Extension

- Have students do more research on the three topics about the city or town they chose.
- Students write a short paper on the city they chose. They can use the text on Istanbul as a model.
- Encourage students to help each other edit their papers in class. Then students revise at home.

Stop and Think! Critical Thinking

What is special about your city or town?

- Remind students of the Warm-up activity in the lesson.
- Students brainstorm things that are special about their city or town in small groups.
- Monitor, offering help as needed.
- When students have finished, have a member from each group go to another group to share their groups' ideas and thoughts.

Wrap-up

Students compare their town or city with another town or city.

- Draw students' attention to the table they completed.
- Ask them to think about how the town or city they live in compares with the one they completed the table about.
- Have students discuss this in small groups. Monitor, offering help as needed.

▥▶ **(No homework today.)**

Preparing for the Next Lesson

Ask students to watch an introduction to folk dancing in India: goo.gl/zjeos5 or invite them to look around on the National Geographic website: goo.gl/7tl2S8.

49

⏱ Culture

Objectives

Students will be able to learn about Indian culture. They will also be able to name things they like about their own country.

Lesson 7   Student's Book p. 48

Warm-up

Students share what they know about a topic to generate interest.

- Draw students' attention to the pictures on pages 48 and 49. Ask them to tell you what they see. Ask students if they recognize anything that they saw in the video.

- Have students share what else they know about India.

> **50**   1 🎧¹⁹ **Listen and write the captions.**

Students are exposed to Indian culture as they match captions to photos.

Answers

top to bottom Henna, Bollywood Movies, The Festival of Holi, Transportation

---

Audio Script

Hi. My name is Shrinivas Naidu and my family is from India. Here are some interesting facts about my country. India is very famous for Bollywood movies. These movies have a lot of music and dancing. There are many forms of transportation in India. Many people don't have cars. This is a picture of a family riding a motorbike. My favorite celebration is the festival of Holi. People throw paint at each other. They use many colors. It's a lot of fun. In India, you might see women with brown henna designs on their hands.

Extension

Have students do some research to learn more about India and its festivals, food and culture. Here is a website to get them started: goo.gl/GEHgiu.

Wrap-up

Students respond to a listening.

- Ask students what they found most interesting about India. Ask *Would you like to travel there? Why or why not?*

- Students form small groups and discuss.

⫸ **(No homework today.)**

Lesson 8   Student's Book pp. 48 and 49

Warm-up
Students review what they've learned.
- Draw students' attention to the photos on page 48.
- Students form pairs and say what's going on in the photos.

2 Read and guess. Circle to complete the sentences.
Students are exposed to some facts about India as they guess which answer correctly completes each sentence.

Answers
1. a, 2. a, 3. b, 4. c, 5. c

3 🎧²⁰ Listen and number the Indian instruments.
Students match the photos of Indian instruments with the sounds they make.

Answers
Left to right 1, 3, 2

Audio Script
1. 5 sec audio sample of Indian sitar music
2. 5 sec audio sample of Indian tabla
3. 5 sec audio sample of Indian flute

4 Read the recipe. What is it similar to?
Students read a recipe for an Indian drink and think about a drink they know of that it is similar to.

Answer
a milkshake / a smoothie

Extension
Make your favorite drink!
- Divide the class into groups. Have students choose a favorite drink and write down the recipe for it. Provide sample language (imperatives) and vocabulary as needed.
- Have students share their recipes with the rest of the class.

Stop and Think! Value
What do you like about your country?
- Students form small groups and discuss what they like about their country.
- Come together as a class and have each group share their thoughts.
- Challenge students to say what they do not like about their country.

Wrap-up
Students reflect on what they have learned.
- Ask students to discuss the following questions in groups of three: *Did any of the information about India surprise you? What kinds of problems do you think a country with so many people might have?* (transportation, housing, education) *Why do you think there are so many languages in India?* (India is a large and old country. A very long time ago, people came to live there from different parts of the world. Each group brought their own language.)

➤ **(No homework today.)**

Project

Lesson 9   Student's Book pp. 50 and 51

Warm-up

Students review the countries they've studied in the unit.

- Show students a map of the world or use the one on page 54.
- Ask students which parts of the world (continents) they've studied in the unit. Elicit *Europe and Asia*. Ask which part they'd like to learn more about and encourage them to explain their answers.

1 Look at the country profile and complete the sentences.

> 52

Students are exposed to some facts about South Africa as they find information in the profile to complete the sentences.

Answers

Flag black, yellow, green, white, red and blue
Capital City Pretoria
Languages 11
Landmarks Cape Town and Table Mountain, Kruger
Traditional Foods bobotie, braaivleis
Popular Sports cricket, rugby, soccer
Wildlife elephants, leopards, lions, rhinoceroses, buffaloes, giraffes, penguins

Wrap-up

Students create a Venn diagram to classify information about countries they've studied in this unit.

- Ask students to think about the countries they've studied: South Africa, Turkey and India.
- Students work in pairs to compare two of the three countries. They use the list of topics that correspond to the texts as support.
- Students make a compare-and-contrast Venn diagram, like this:

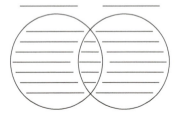

- Show students how to complete the Venn diagram: Write the names of the countries on the top blanks, for example, *South Africa* and *India*. Below *South Africa*, write facts about the country in the circle; below *India*, write facts about the country in that circle. Where the circles meet, write what the two countries have in common.
- Display students' Venn diagrams in the classroom.

 (No homework today.)

Teaching Tip

Using Graphic Organizers

Graphic organizers can help students process information and serve as a visual aid for students. You can use a graphic organizer before, during or after an activity. For example, an effective graphic organizer to use before and after an activity, to generate interest, is a KWL chart. A KWL page is divided into three headings: What do I **k**now? What do I **w**ant to know? What did I **l**earn? Students access prior knowledge by answering the first two questions; they reflect on what they've learned by answering the last question. Students can use graphic organizers to help them with projects and homework, or as part of their review for tests. There are many kinds of graphic organizers, including diagrams, charts and maps. Here is a link to some useful graphic organizers: goo.gl/hUhwcW.

Warm-up

Students brainstorm countries.

- Tell students to think of countries that they are interested in. List some countries on the board.

- Have students say what they know about the countries and why they are interesting.

2 Choose a country and make a country profile.

Students make a country profile.

- Draw students' attention to the profile of South Africa. Review the topics that are covered by going over the sentences in Activity 1.

- Students choose a country and make a profile of it. You may wish to have the class decide on three or four countries and then have the class form groups to do the project.

- Display the profiles in the classroom.

The Digital Touch

To incorporate digital media in the project, suggest one or more of the following:

- Students can use the Internet to do research on their country of choice. Ask students to tell the class the search words they used and which got them the best results.

- Students can prepare a presentation of their country profiles using PowerPoint or free software like Google Slides.

Note that students should have the option to do a task on paper or digitally.

Wrap-up

Students share their country profiles.

- Give students some time to look at their presentations and make notes similar to the sentences in Activity 1.

- Have students present their profiles to whole the class or in small groups.

▮▮▶ **Workbook p. 136, Activities 1 and 2 (Review)**

 **Review**

Objective

Students will be able to consolidate their understanding of the vocabulary and grammar learned in the unit.

Lesson 11   Student's Book p. 52

✔ **Homework Check!**

Workbook p. 136, Activities 1 and 2

Answers

1 Complete the nationality words.

1. French, 2. Brazilian, 3. Peruvian, 4. Italian,
5. Turkish, 6. Japanese, 7. Thai, 8. Australian,
9. British, 10. Egyptian, 11. Greek, 12. American,
13. Chinese

2 Read and choose the correct option.

1. 're, 2. can, 3. can, 4. are, 5. are, 6. are, 7. is, 8. 's

▶ 54

Warm-up

Students list the vocabulary and grammar they have learned in the unit.

• Ask students to think of what they've learned in this unit.

• Elicit and list the grammar and vocabulary on the board. Vocabulary: countries and nationalities *(Australia / Australian, Brazil / Brazilian, China / Chinese, Egypt / Egyptian, France / French, Greece / Greek, India / Indian, Italy / Italian, Japan / Japanese, Peru / Peruvian, Thailand / Thai, Turkey / Turkish, The United Kingdom [The UK] / British, The United States [The US] / American)*. Grammar: *the verb* be, and *the modal* can.

1 Look and complete the country names. Then write the nationalities.

Students complete the country name that goes with each photo and write the corresponding nationality.

Answers

1. United Kingdom, British, 2. Peru, Peruvian,
3. India, Indian, 4. Australia, Australian,
5. United States, American, 6. Egypt, Egyptian,
7. China, Chinese, 8. Brazil, Brazilian

2 Classify the words. Then complete the table.

Students identify whether each word is a country or a nationality and complete the table accordingly.

Answers

Country France, Greece, Italy, Japan,
Thailand, Turkey
Nationality French, Greek, Italian, Japanese,
Thai, Turkish

Wrap-up

Students practice countries and nationalities vocabulary.

• Form small groups. Have students look at the pictures in Activity 1. Tell them to take turns, choosing one of the countries and say, for example, *I'm from Egypt*. The other two students race to say the corresponding nationality: *You're Egyptian!* Students continue until they've talked about all the pictures.

• Challenge students to say sentences with other countries and nationalities they know.

 (No homework today.)

Lesson 12 · Student's Book p. 53

Warm-up

Students play a guessing game to review countries and nationalities.

- Tell students they will play a guessing game. You give clues and students guess, e.g., Say *I'm thinking of a country. It starts with F. (France), The capital of this country is Pretoria. (South Africa), This animal can climb trees. (Giant panda),* etc.

3 Look and write the sentences.

Students write affirmative (✓) and negative (✗) sentences using cues and the verb *be*.

Answers

1. The capital of India is not / isn't Mumbai.
2. Tokyo is the capital of Japan. 3. Rome and Venice are Italian cities. 4. Cairo is not / isn't the capital of Peru. 5. New York and Boston are in the United States.

4 Read and complete the information card.

Students practice the verb *be* and the modal *can* by completing sentences.

Answers

top to bottom are, can, can, can

5 Look and write the contractions.

Students write contractions of *be*.

Answers

1. aren't, 2. They're, 3. isn't, 4. It's, 5. can't

Big Question

Students are given the opportunity to revisit the Big Question and reflect on it.

- Ask students to turn to the unit opener on page 41 and think about the discussion they had in the Warm-up in Lesson 1 about their own country(ies).

- Ask students to think of other activities they've done and discussions they've had about where they're from: see the Lesson 3 Warm-up, Lesson 6 Warm-up and Wrap-up, Lesson 8 Stop and Think! and Lesson 11 Stop and Think! and Wrap-up.

- Students form small groups and discuss the following:
  - » What's the best thing about your country: the food, landmarks, wildlife, cultural life (for example, festivals), sports?
  - » What are some things you don't always like about your country: traffic, economy, schools, pollution?
  - » Have you visited any of the places in the unit, or know someone who has? What is the place like? How does it compare to your country?

⭐ Scorecard

Hand out (and/or project) a *Scorecard*. Have students fill in their *Scorecards* for this unit.

⟼ **Study for the unit test.**

4 What is home?

Grammar
There is / are: <u>There's</u> a table in the kitchen.
Where: <u>Where</u> is the cat?
Prepositions of place: *beetween, in front of, on, in, next to*: There are books <u>on</u> the table.
Short answers: No, there aren't.

Vocabulary
Rooms: bathroom, bedroom, dining room, kitchen, laundry room, living room, closet
House Objects: bed, chair, dryer, refrigerator (fridge), shower, sink, sofa, stove, table, television (TV), toilet, washer

Listening
Looking at photos and making predictions

Reading
Reading about statistics

What is home?

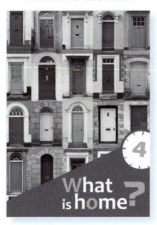

In the first lesson, read the unit title aloud and have students look carefully at the unit cover. Encourage them to think about the message in the picture. At the end of the unit, students will discuss the big question: *What is home?*

 Teaching Tip

Activating Students' Prior Knowledge

Successful learning relates new information to what we already know. By activating what students already know, you can help with the learning process. Here are some quick tips to follow: Your Warm-up can be a diagnostic tool. If you find that your students don't know quite as much as you'd thought, you may choose to adjust the new language you want to teach. Use specific tools, such as graphic organizers and brainstorming sessions, to get your students thinking about what they know. Think carefully about how you pair and group students. It may make sense to have a student with more prior knowledge, with more confidence, with a student who is less proficient. Most importantly, be flexible. If you have to adapt your lesson some, be ready. If you have to change group members, don't be afraid to call a time-out and do so.

 **Vocabulary**

Objective
Students will be able to use **rooms** and **house objects** vocabulary to talk about their homes.

Lesson 1   Student's Book pp. 56 and 57

Warm-up
Students discuss what home is.
- Draw students' attention to the unit opener page. Say *Look at the doors of the homes. What's behind them?*
- Have students form small groups and talk about the rooms and things inside a house. Allow them to talk freely, noting what vocabulary and structures they already know.

1 **²¹ Listen and complete.**
Students learn house objects vocabulary while they listen for the spelling.
- Draw students' attention to the **Guess What!** box. Read the information aloud. Point out that *TV* is like the other short forms: *TV* comes from the letters in *television*. Explain that *fridge* is a shorter way to say *refrigerator*.

Answers

top to bottom refrigerator, stove, television, washer, dryer, table, bed, sofa, chair, sink, shower, toilet

Audio Script
Appliances
That's a refrigerator! R-E-F-R-I-G-E-R-A-T-O-R.
That's a stove. S-T-O-V-E.
That's a washer. W-A-S-H-E-R.
That's a dryer. D-R-Y-E-R.

Furniture
That's a table! T-A-B-L-E.
That's a bed! B-E-D.
That's a sofa! S-O-F-A.
That's a chair! C-H-A-I-R.

Fixtures
That's a sink! S-I-N-K.
That's a shower! S-H-O-W-E-R.
That's a toilet! T-O-I-L-E-T.

2 **Read and number the rooms.**
Students read the sentences and match each one with the photo of the room.
Answers

left to right, top to bottom 2, 6, 5, 3, 4, 1

Extension
Students have a spelling bee to practice the new vocabulary: appliances, furniture, fixtures and rooms.
- Students form two or three teams. Each team stands in different parts of the classroom.
- Give one of the vocabulary words to a student, alternating teams. If the student spells the word correctly, she goes to the end of the line until her turn comes up again. If she spells the word incorrectly, she sits down. The last team standing wins.

Wrap-up
Students draw pictures of their homes in their vocabulary notebooks.
- Model the activity by drawing a quick sketch of one of the rooms in your home. Describe a room. For example, say *This is my bedroom. I have a bed, a table and a chair.*
- Students form pairs or groups of three and take turns describing their homes to each other. Monitor, offering help as needed.

➡ **Workbook p. 138, Activity 1**

58

✔ **Homework Check!**

Workbook p. 138, Activity 1

Answers

1 Look and unscramble.

2. refrigerator, 3. toilet, 4. sofa, 5. dryer, 6. chair,
7. table, 8. sink, 9. television, 10. shower,
11. stove, 12. washer

Warm-up

Students play a game to review rooms vocabulary.

- Model the activity. Mime an action you do in a room in a house, for example, yawn and pretend to sleep. Ask, *Which room am I in?* Elicit the bedroom.

- Students take turns miming actions and guessing the room.

3 🎧²² Listen and write the room.

Students identify the room based on actions they hear.

Answers

1. living room, 2. bathroom, 3. kitchen,
4. laundry room, 5. dining room, 6. bedroom

Audio Script

1. SFX changing channels on a TV
2. SFX toilet flushing
3. SFX chopping vegetables
4. SFX washer filling, door shutting, starting
5. SFX clinking of dishes while eating
6. SFX bedroom – person snoring, alarm clock starts beeping

4 Look and match.

Students match photos of items associated with house objects.

Answers

left to right 2, 4, 5, 1, 3

5 Think Fast! Look and identify the room.

Students do a thirty-second timed challenge: they identify rooms based on items you find in them.

Answers

1. living room, 2. bathroom, 3. bathroom,
4. bedroom, 5. kitchen, 6. laundry room, 7. kitchen,
8. dining room

Extension

- Students play a game of Go Fish!
- Make sets of cards, or have students make them. Write each house object on a card, and write the corresponding room for each object on another card. For example, for the three cards *sink*, *shower* and *toilet*, make three cards that all say *bathroom*.
- Students form pairs. Give each group a set of cards. Student put all the cards in the middle of the desk or table. This is the "pond." Both students take five cards from the pond. They lay down any pairs they have (a pair is an object with the room that corresponds to the object).
- Students take turns asking for corresponding cards to make pairs. A student who has an object asks for the corresponding room: *Do you have the kitchen?* And a student who has a room asks for an object: *Do you have a sink?* If the other student has that card, he / she gives it to him. If the student doesn't have the card, he / she says *Go fish.* The partner then draws a card from the pond and lays down any pairs.
- The game continues until all cards are paired up. The students with the most pairs is the winner.

Wrap-up

Students review house objects vocabulary.

- Draw students' attention to the photos of the rooms in Activity 2 and the icons in Activity 1.
- Model the activity with a student. Say *I can see a table and four chairs. I can eat in this room. What is it?* Elicit *It's a dining room.*
- Students form pairs and take turns describing and guessing rooms. Monitor, offering help as needed.

➠ **Workbook p. 138, Activity 2**

🐝 Teaching Tip

Limiting New Vocabulary in Each Lesson

Students need to read or hear a new word ten to fifteen times to learn it effectively. So more exposure, rather than more vocabulary, is key. If you want your students to learn—really learn—new vocabulary, you should limit your word list to around ten <u>new</u> words per lesson. When the vocabulary set has words that are most likely known to students already, you can include a few more.

Grammar

Objective
Students will be able to use ***there is / there are, where*** and ***prepositions*** to talk about objects in houses.

Lesson 3   Student's Book pp. 58 and 59

> ✔ **Homework Check!**
>
> Workbook p. 138, Activity 2
>
> **Answers**
>
> **2 Look and label the rooms.**
> 1. kitchen, 2. bedroom, 3. living room,
> 4. bathroom, 5. dining room

Warm-up
Students review house objects vocabulary.
- Draw students' attention to the photos on pages 58 and 59. Ask *What can you see?* Write a few items on the board.
- Set a stopwatch for one minute. Students race the clock to list as many things as they can. Encourage them to use the new vocabulary.

1 Read and number the objects in the pictures.
Students are exposed to *there is / isn't* and
there are / aren't while practicing vocabulary.
- Point out the word order in the sentences: *There is* or *There are* followed by a noun phrase.
- Draw students' attention to the ***There is / are*** box and explain the singular, plural and negative forms.

Answers

Left to right, top to bottom 4, 5, 3, 1, 7, 6, 2

2 Read and complete the description.
Students complete a text describing photos using affirmative and negative forms of the verb *be*.

Answers

1. isn't, 2. is, 3. are, 4. is, 5. is, 6. aren't

Wrap-up
Students answer questions about things in photos to review *there is / are*.
- Hold up the photos or bring in some other photos.
- Ask questions with *there are*. Be sure to ask some that will elicit a negative response, for example, *Is there a washer in the kitchen?* Elicit *No, there isn't.*
- Challenge students to ask questions, too.

➡ **Workbook p. 139, Activities 1–3**

Student's Book pp. 58 and 59

✔ **Homework Check!**

Workbook p. 139, Activities 1–3

Answers

1 Complete the sentences using 's or are.
1. 's, 2. are, 3. are, 4. 's
2 Read and underline. Then match.
1. <u>a plant</u>, <u>It</u>'s very big. 2. <u>two chairs</u>, <u>They</u>'re very comfortable. 3. <u>a photo</u>, <u>It</u>'s very special.
3 Look and write the correct preposition.
1. between, 2. between, 3. on

Warm-up

Students review the rules for using *there is* and *there are*.

- Students form small groups. Tell groups to take out a piece of paper and write the contraction for each form of *there is / there are* that you say. If you say something that doesn't have a contraction, have students write an (✗) next to that number. 1. *there is,* 2. *there are,* 3. *there is not,* 4. *there are not.*

Answers

1. *there's,* 2. ✗, 3. *there isn't,* 4. *there aren't*

---

3 Circle the correct option. Then complete the answers.
Students practice questions and short answers with *there is / are*.

Answers

1. Is, 2. Is, there, 3. Is, there is, 4. Is, there isn't, 5. Are, there are, 6. Are, aren't

---

4 Read and match.
Students match questions with *Where* to the correct answer using prepositions.

- Draw students' attention to the **Guess What!** box. Read the information aloud. Go over the word order of questions with *Where*: *Where,* followed by *is / are,* followed by noun or noun phrase.

- Elicit the prepositions of place from Unit 2: *on, under, next to* and *in.* Present *in front of* and *between*: stand in front of the board and say *I'm in front of the board*; stand between two chairs and say *I'm between two chairs.* Draw pictures like these on the board:

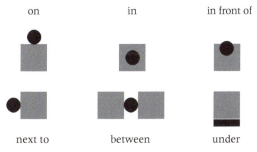

| on | in | in front of |
| next to | between | under |

Answers

1. It's in front of the window. 2. They're on the fridge. 3. It's on the bed. 4. They're on the wall.

---

5 Think Fast! **In your notebook, write ten sentences to describe your house.**
Students do a three-minute timed challenge: they personalize the vocabulary and grammar by writing sentences that describe their own houses.

Answers

Answers will vary.

Extension

- Students take out the pictures of their homes. Students form pairs and sit back to back. They have to describe a room in their home to their partners and their partners have to draw that room.

- Students can ask questions for accuracy: *Where is the sofa? It's next to the door.*

- Students continue until they've finished drawing a room. Then they show each other their pictures and compare. If time allows and students are engaged, they can continue with other rooms.

Wrap-up

Students review *there is, there are* and questions with *Where.*

- Tell students to imagine their bedroom, as it is. Then tell them to imagine that it's completely empty: no furniture, no toys or games, nothing. Tell them to think about their perfect, dream bedrooms. What furniture do they want to have? Where will it be? What other objects do they want to have in their rooms?

- Students form pairs and describe their ideal bedrooms. Monitor, offering help as needed.

➡ **Workbook pp. 139 and 140, Activities 4–6**

⏱ *Listening & Reading*

Objectives

Students will be able to look at photos and make predictions. They will also be able to read about statistics.

Lesson 5 — Student's Book **p. 60**

> ✔ **Homework Check!**
>
> Workbook pp. 139 and 140, Activities 4–6
>
> **Answers**
>
> **4 In your notebook, write the negative forms of the sentences.**
>
> 1. There isn't a chair in the laundry room. 2. There aren't any magnets on the fridge. 3. There isn't a closet in the bedroom. 4. There aren't any books on the table.
>
> **5 Write questions. Then look and answer.**
>
> 1. Is there a television in the bedroom? No, there isn't. 2. Are there any magnets on the fridge? Yes, there are. 3. Is there a lamp in the living room? Yes, there is.
>
> **6 Complete the questions and answers.**
>
> 1. are, on the, 2. is, It's in the, 3. are, They're in the

Warm-up

Students think about what home means to generate interest.

- Write the letters HOME on the board vertically (↓). Explain that students will write a poem about home called *an acrostic*. Model the activity by writing your own poem:

  Happy place

  Open doors for all

  My family

  Enjoying a place to relax

- Students write H-O-M-E vertically to write their poem. When students have finished, have them share their poems with the class. If time permits, they can draw pictures and decorate their poems.

1 🎧²³ Listen and write *D* (Debbie), *A* (Aaron) or *M* (Miles).

Students identify homes based on descriptions in a listening.

- Draw students' attention to the **Be Strategic!** box. Read the information aloud, look at the photos and make predictions by answering the questions.

Answers

Top to bottom M, D, A

Audio Script

Miles: For me, home is about family. I live in the windmill with my three kids. It's old and there aren't many windows, but we like it. We have a small farm, too.

Aaron: I'm Aaron. I live in a houseboat on a lake. It's very big, with a lot of windows. There are plants, too. I think home is a place to relax and escape from problems.

Debbie: I'm Debbie. I work a lot, so home is just a place to sleep, really. My mobile home isn't big or elegant, but there's enough space for me and my two cats.

2 🎧²³ Listen again and identify the person.

Students listen closely for specific information. They match each sentence with the speaker.

Answers

Top to bottom Debbie, Aaron, Miles

Wrap-up

Students discuss their reactions to a listening.

- Draw students' attention to the three quotes in Activity 2 and to the poems students wrote in the Warm-up.

- Ask *What is home to you? Is it family, a place to relax or just a place to sleep?*

- Don't worry about accuracy. Let students share their thoughts.

⏩ **(No homework today.)**

Warm-up

Students brainstorm other features of homes.

- Ask students to list the vocabulary for homes they've learned so far. Write these categories on the board: *furniture, fixtures, appliances, rooms.*

- Students brainstorm other words to talk about homes: *types of homes* (a house, an apartment, a condo, a duplex, a bungalow, a mobile home, a houseboat, a lighthouse, a tent), *other features* (a garage, a yard, a lawn, a garden, an outdoor playset, a swimming pool, a balcony / porch, a gazebo, a shed).

- Ask students to say how common these things are in their neighborhoods.

3 Read and guess the answers. Then compare with a classmate.

Students guess statistics about US homes.

4 🎧²⁴ Listen and check.

Students listen to statistics about US homes and compare the answers with their guesses in Activity 3.

Answers

left to right 80, 66, 64, 55, 31

Audio Script

Eighty percent of houses have a garage.
Sixty-six percent of homeowners have children.
Sixty-four percent of houses have a dining room.
Fifty-five percent of homeowners have pets.
Thirty-one percent of houses have two or more bathrooms.

Stop and Think! Critical Thinking

What makes a place into a home?

- Remind students of the physical features of places where people live, in houses, apartments or other types of homes.

- Ask students to think about the words *a house* and *a home*. Ask, *Is there a difference between a house and a home? What makes a place into a home?*

- Students form small groups to discuss. Monitor, offering help as needed, but don't focus on accuracy. Just let students express their thoughts freely.

Wrap-up

Students compare their homes with typical homes in the US.

- Draw students' attention to the completed graph.

- Tell students some other facts about US households, for example,

  » *Sixty-three percent of people own their homes; thirty-seven percent rent.*

  » *Eighty percent of all American houses have lawns.*

  » *Thirty percent of water used on the east coast of the US goes toward watering those lawns.*

  » *About twenty-five percent of people live with "extended families," which includes grandparents, aunts and uncles and other extended family members.*

- Ask *How does your home compare with homes in the US?* Students form small groups and compare their countries with the US in every category.

▶ **Workbook p. 141, Activities 1 and 2**

 63 ◀

Preparing for the Next Lesson

Ask students to watch an introduction to nomads in Mongolia: goo.gl/RH57b0 or invite them to look around on the website: goo.gl/0rxpAs.

Culture

Objective

Students will be able to talk about the Tuareg. They will also be able to discuss what we can learn from their way of life.

Lesson 7 Student's Book pp. 62 and 63

> ✔ **Homework Check!**
>
> Workbook p. 141, Activities 1 and 2
>
> **Answers**
> **1 Read and number the descriptions.**
> *top to bottom* 3, 1, 2
>
> **2 Read the descriptions again and complete the table.**
> 1. in a forest, quiet; 2. big, in the countryside, luxurious; 3. very small, in the city, modern

Warm-up

Students make a KWL chart to generate interest in a text.

- Draw students' attention to the photo. Ask them what they can see. Explain that these countries are part of the world that is called *North Africa*.

- Write the letters K, W and L on the board. Draw vertical lines between the letters.

- Ask *What do you know about North Africa and deserts?* Students complete the first column: what they know.

- Then ask *What do you want to know?* Students complete the second column: what they want to know.

1 Look and circle the correct option.

Students predict information about a reading by choosing the correct word to complete each sentence.

Answers

1. Africa, 2. desert, 3. tents, 4. camels, 5. hot

2 Read the text and complete the sentences.

Students read a paragraph about a nomadic group, the Tuareg, and complete sentences with information from the text.

- Draw students' attention to the **Guess What!** box. Read the information aloud. Explain or elicit that *racial characteristics* are things like eye color, hair color, skin tone and height. Ask them to notice the characteristics of the boy in the photo. Ask students what kind of racial characteristics people from their country have. Elicit answers from the whole class.

Answers

1. Sahara, 2. six, 3. million, 4. camel, 5. turbans

Wrap-up

Students add to their KWL charts.

- Have students take out their KWL charts. Students read what they wrote, focusing on the W column.

- Ask, *What did you learn from the reading? Did you learn some of the things you wanted to? Do you want to learn anything more?*

- Students add what they learned to the W column on their KWL charts.

➠ **(No homework today.)**

Warm-up

Students review what they've learned.

- Write the words and figures on the board: *Tuaregs, Sahara, six, two million, tent, turbans.*

- Ask students to tell you what they refer to. Elicit or provide answers similar to the following: *Tuaregs are the name of a nomads in Northern Aftrica. Sahara is the desert where the Tuareg people live. Six is the number of countries where they live and move around. Two million is how many Tuaregs there are. Tuaregs live in tents and the men wear cloths called turbans on their heads.*

- Have students take out their KWL charts from last class. Encourage them to share some of the things they learned from the reading and say what they still want to learn.

3 🎧²⁵ **Listen and number the photos.**

Students listen to more information about the Tuareg and number the photos to correspond with the order each item is mentioned in the audio.

Answers

From top to bottom 3, 5, 2, 1, 4

Audio Script

1. The Tuareg are experts at desert survival. They often travel at night when it is not hot. They use the stars to navigate.
2. They use camels—perfect transportation, because camels can survive for a long time without food or water.
3. The Tuareg wear turbans to protect them from the hot sun and the sand.
4. They drink lots of mint tea to stay alert.
5. The Tuareg can grow food in an oasis.

Extension

Tell students to imagine that they have just spent a week living and traveling with the Tuareg people. Ask them to think about these questions:

- Where do you sleep?
- What is the weather like?
- What do you wear?
- How do you get around?
- What do you drink?
- What do you eat? (They will have to use their imaginations or do some research to answer this.)
- What are the people like?
- Was it a good experience? Why or why not?
- Students write a postcard to a friend or family member telling him or her about the experience. Display the postcards in the classroom.

Stop and Think! Value

What are the advantages and disadvantages of the Tuareg way of life? What can we learn from them?

- Read the information in the box. Students form pairs. They take a few minutes to make notes of advantages and disadvantages of the Tuareg way of life.

- Students form small groups to discuss their lists and the question *What can we learn from the Tuareg way of life?*

Wrap-up

Students react to what they've learned and complete their KWL charts.

- Have students take out their KWL charts. Ask them to think about what they've learned from the text, the listening and the discussions they have had about the Tuareg people.

- Students add to and complete their KWL charts.

- Students form small groups to discuss the information in their charts and their thoughts on the reading and listening.

▪▪▶ **(No homework today.)**

 **Project**

Objectives
Students will be able to design a home.

Lesson 9   Student's Book pp. 64 and 65

Warm-up
Students review types of houses to generate interest.
- Draw students' attention to the three houses on page 60.
- Ask students what kind of houses they are: *a windmill, a mobile home, a houseboat.* Ask students to recall some of the other types of homes they've discussed throughout the unit. Write some on the board: *apartment, bungalow, tent, condo,* etc.
- Have students work in small groups. Tell them to choose three types of home and create lists of pros (advantages) and cons (disadvantages) of each type of home.

 66

1 Look at page 65 and mark (✓) the features of the home design.
Students are exposed to other types of homes while they identify the features of the example of a home design.

Answers
Type of Home a houseboat, *Location* in the city, *Style* casual, *Decorations* plants and flowers

2 Design a home using the characteristics in Activity 1. Describe the furniture, fixtures and appliances.
Students use what they've learned about houses during the unit to design their own homes.

> **The Digital Touch**
> To incorporate digital media in the project, suggest one or more of the following:
> - Encourage students to make their homes more eco-friendly. They can visit this website to see how their choices affect the "green" rating of their homes: goo.gl/J10jNx.
> - Students create a 3-D floor plan of their home: goo.gl/VZilha.
>
> Note that students should have the option to do a task on paper or digitally.

Wrap-up
Students consolidate what they've learned.
- Draw students' attention to the three houses on page 60 again.
- Students form pairs and describe the houses using the language from the unit. Explain to students that this exercise will help them prepare for giving presentations on their homes.

Teaching Tip
Helping Students Give Successful Presentations
It's important that students are prepared for in-class presentations. The more prepared they are, the more successful and less nervous they will be. Here are some things for students to consider: make sure students understand what they're going to talk about. In this case, they will present their ideal home. Encourage them to say why they want certain features, what they want to do in each room and how the feature will enable them to do that. Keep the required speaking-time short. Leave this part up to your students, but tell them they have to use at least one visual aid: a map, a poster, a photo. Encourage students to make notes. Finally, tell students to speak loudly, clearly and slowly.

Warm-up

Students think of questions to ask the presenters.

- As a class or in small groups, brainstorm questions to ask the presenters, for example, *Why do you want [a bathroom] there? How will you decorate your home? Who will you live with?*

- Write some questions on the board for students to refer to during the presentations.

- Give students some time to go over their presentations.

3 Present your design to the class.

Students share their designs with the class.

- Students present, one by one, to the class. Either have students come up in alphabetical order or have them draw numbers, so the order is objective.

- Tell students that they must be quiet and listen politely when other students are presenting. Encourage them to try to think of at least one question to ask the person presenting.

- When each student has finished presenting, be sure to ask the others if there are any questions.

Extension

- Hold a contest for students, in your class and other classes, to vote on your students' designs.
- Have different categories: The most comfortable home, the most innovative, the most eco-friendly, the most casual, the most modern, etc.

The Digital Touch

To incorporate digital media in the project, suggest one or more of the following:

- Students can make a PowerPoint presentation to present their designs to the class.
- Students can use some new digital presentation techniques to present their designs. Here is a list of some new digital presentation tools: goo.gl/Na4QLL.

Note that students should have the option to do a task on paper or digitally.

Wrap-up

Students reflect on their presentations.

- Ask students to think about the following questions:
  - » *What went well with my presentation?*
  - » *Did I prepare and practice enough?*
  - » *What didn't go very well?*
  - » *How can I improve for the next presentation?*

- Students form small groups to discuss.

⇒ Workbook p. 140, Activity 1 (Review)

 **Review**

Objective

Students will be able to consolidate their understanding of the vocabulary and grammar learned in the unit.

Lesson 11 Student's Book pp. 66 and 67

✔ **Homework Check!**

Workbook p. 140, Activity 1 (Review)

Answers

1 In your notebook, correct the sentences.

1. ~~aren't~~ There <u>isn't</u> a television in the kitchen.
2. ~~isn't~~ There <u>aren't</u> chairs in the bedroom.
3. ~~in bathroom~~ Is there a shower in <u>the</u> bathroom?
4. ~~photos are~~ Where <u>are</u> <u>the</u> <u>photos</u>?

Warm-up

Students list the vocabulary and grammar they have learned in the unit.

- Ask students to think of what they've learned in this unit.
- Elicit and list the grammar and vocabulary on the board. Vocabulary: Rooms: *bathroom, bedroom, dining room, kitchen, laundry room, living room;* House objects: *bed, chair, dryer, refrigerator, shower, sink, sofa, stove, table, television, toilet, washer.* Grammar: *there is / there are,* prepositions: *between, in front of, on, in, next to.*

1 Look and label the rooms.

Students label photos with the room shown in each.

Answers

1. living room, 2. bedroom, 3. dining room,
4. laundry room, 5. kitchen, 6. bathroom

2 Look and circle the correct option.

Students choose the correct word for each icon of a house object.

Answers

1. lamp, 2. toilet, 3. shower, 4. bed, 5. chair

3 Look, read and mark (✓) the correct description.

Students identify the correct description of a room shown in a photo.

Answers

There's a sink and a stove. There are two chairs. There's a refrigerator.

Wrap-up

Students review vocabulary and grammar by describing photos of rooms.

- Refer students to the descriptions on pages 64 and 65.
- Students form pairs and take turns describing the photos in Activity 1. Encourage them to use the vocabulary from the lesson, *there is / there are* and prepositions.

 (No homework today.)

Warm-up

Students remember what they reviewed in the previous lesson.

- Ask students what they've reviewed. Elicit *rooms and house objects vocabulary*.

- Ask students to say what they will be reviewing today. Elicit *there is / there are* and *prepositions*.

◄ **Look and write the prepositions.**

Students complete phrases with the correct preposition to describe where the cat is.

Answers

1. in front of, 2. on, 3. between, 4. in, 5. next to

5 Look and complete the sentences.

Students complete sentences describing a picture with the correct forms of *there is* and *there are*.

Answers

1. There is, 2. There are, 3. There is, 4. There aren't, 5. There is, 6. There aren't

6 Unscramble the questions.

Students review word order of questions with *there is* and *there are*.

Answers

1. Is there a shower in the bathroom? 2. Are there plates on the table? 3. Is there a dryer in the laundry room? 4. Is there a fridge in the kitchen?

? Big Question

Students are given the opportunity to revisit the Big Question and reflect on it.

- Ask students to turn to the unit opener on page 55 and think about the discussion they had in the Warm-up in Lesson 1.

- Ask students to think of other activities they've done and discussions they've had about home: Lesson 5 Warm-up, the listening and Wrap-up; Lesson 6 Stop and Think! Ask them to think about the designs of their perfect homes.

- Students form small groups and discuss the following:
  » What makes a happy home?
  » Is the size of a home important? Why or why not?
  » There's an expression "There's no place like home." Do you agree? Why or why not?
  » What do you think these expressions mean? *a home away from home, homesick, make yourself at home*.
  » How do you imagine your homes when you are older and independent?

 Scorecard

Hand out (and/or project) a *Scorecard*. Have students fill in their *Scorecards* for this unit.

⏭ **Study for the unit test.**

5 What's your routine?

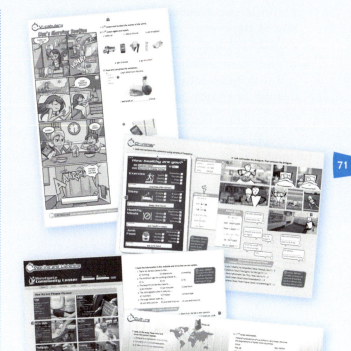

Grammar

Adverbs of frequency: I <u>always</u> wake up at seven thirty. We <u>never</u> eat junk food. She <u>sometimes</u> eats a big breakfast.

Present simple: He <u>eats</u> dinner at six o'clock. She <u>doesn't</u> <u>watch</u> TV in the morning. <u>Do</u> they <u>go</u> to the gym after school? Yes, they <u>do</u>. / No, they <u>don't</u>.

Vocabulary

Routines: brush my teeth, do homework, get dressed, go to bed, go to school, eat breakfast / lunch / dinner, take a shower, wake up

Time: six o'clock (six a.m. / p.m.), six (oh) five, a quarter past six, half past six (six thirty), a quarter to seven

Reading

Reading a timetable

Listening

Thinking about questions other people will ask you

What's your routine?

In the first lesson, read the unit title aloud and have students look carefully at the unit cover. Encourage them to think about the message in the picture. At the end of the unit, students will discuss the big question: *What's your routine?*

Teaching Tip

Using Games in the Classroom

Games can help encourage and sustain students' interest in a topic. They also allow teachers to create contexts in which the use of language is useful and meaningful. When using games in the classroom, remember that games don't always have to be competitive, they can also be cooperative; a game should keep all the students involved and interested, it should give students the chance to learn, practice or review specific language material and it should enable students to focus on the use of the language rather than on the language itself. Games should be central to your teaching, and not just used as time fillers.

Vocabulary

Lesson 1   Student's Book pp. 70 and 71

Warm-up

Students start thinking about the Big Question.

- Draw students' attention to the title of the unit. Read it aloud and ask *What's your routine?* Explain that *a routine* is something you do every day or on certain days regularly.

- Draw students' attention to the photos on page 69. Ask *Do you do the things in the pictures?* Elicit answers, but don't worry about accuracy here.

- In pairs, have students discuss what they see. Use this as an opportunity to check what vocabulary and structures your students already know.

1 🎧²⁶ **Listen and number the scenes of the comic.**

Students number the frames of the comic strip according to the order of events in the audio.

 72

Answers

top to bottom 4, 1, 3, 2

Audio Script

LISA: Hi! I'm Lisa and this is my morning routine. I wake up at—
MOM: Lisa! Time for school!
LISA: I wake up at six o'clock.
LISA: Then I take a sh— There's no hot water!
LISA: Then I take a shower.
LISA: Then I eat breakfast. Jimmy!
JIMMY: Oops. Sorry!
LISA: Then I get dressed—
MOM: Hurry up, Lisa!
LISA: At seven o'clock I get on the bus and go to school.

2 🎧²⁶ **Listen again and match.**

Students match photos of items with the routines they correspond to.

Answers

left to right 5, 1, 4, 2, 3

Wrap-up

Students personalize the topic.

- Draw students' attention to the comic strip. Ask *Is your morning routine like Lisa's?*

- In pairs, have students discuss their morning routines. If time permits, have pairs share with the class how their routines are similar or different.

▶ Workbook p. 142, Activity 1

✔ **Homework Check!**

Workbook p. 142, Activity 1

Answers

1 Look and complete.

1. wake, 2. breakfast, 3. dressed, 4. a shower,
5. school, 6. eat / have, 7. dinner, 8. homework,
9. go to

Warm-up

Students review actions.

• Model the activity by miming one of the actions from the comic strip. For example, *take a shower*.

• The first student who guesses correctly comes to the front of the class to mime another action. The student who guesses that action comes up and mimes yet a third action. Continue until all actions have been mimed and guessed or as long as students are engaged.

3 Read and complete the sentences.

Students complete sentences about routines with the appropriate times.

Answers

1. one, 2. school, 3. six, 4. thirty

4 Think Fast! In your notebook, write eight sentences about your routine.

Students do a five-minute timed challenge: they write about their routines to personalize vocabulary.

• Draw students' attention to the **Guess What!** box. Read the information aloud.

• Have students add *a.m.* and *p.m.* as appropriate to their sentences.

Answers

Answers will vary.

Extension

Students make a mind map of their daily activities.

• Students draw their mind maps. The center circle reads *My daily activities*. There are four circles coming off the center circle: *morning, evening, during the day, other.*

• Students refer to the vocabulary and the reading to complete their mind maps.

Wrap-up

Students use vocabulary in context.

• Students form pairs to talk about their routines. Encourage them to use *a.m.* and *p.m.* Monitor, offering help as needed.

• For more practice, have students form new pairs.

• If time allows, have a few students report to the class the routine of another student in the class.

▶ **Workbook p, 142, Activity 2**

🐝 **Teaching Tip**

Keeping Students Engaged

Getting all students involved in activities is not always easy. Think about the learning environment and try to incorporate more ways to encourage students to get involved in class activities. Provide opportunities for students to build fluency. The more students practice speaking, the more confident they will become. Do your best to choose or modify activities that interest your students. Providing context goes a long way in engaging your students. Think about individual needs when possible. When you talk to a student, allow enough time for the student to respond. Sometimes this seems like a long time to you, but the student may need time to gather his or her thoughts.

 **Grammar**

Objective

Students will be able to use **adverbs of frequency** and **present simple** to talk about habits, schedules and routines.

Lesson 3   Student's Book p. 72

> ✔ **Homework Check!**
>
> Workbook page 142, Activity 2
>
> **Answers**
> **2 Look and write the times.**
> 1. half past ten, 2. quarter to three, 3. quarter past nine, 4. ten oh five

Warm-up

Students review the days of the week.

- Have students stand in two rows, forming two teams.
- The first pair of students walks to the front of the class. Say a prompt about a day of the week, for example, *The day before Monday is* …. Students respond as quickly as possible then go to the back of the line or sit down.

 74

- Continue with prompts such as *The day after Thursday is … The day between Wednesday and Friday is … The first day of the week is … The last day of the weekend is …*

1 Look and complete the comments using adverbs of frequency.

Students complete sentences with the correct adverbs of frequency according to the number of days marked for each activity.

- Draw students' attention to the *Adverbs of Frequency* box. Review the information in the chart. Confirm students understand the meaning of *always, sometimes* and *never*.
- Also draw students' attention to the *Guess What!* box. Read the information aloud.

Answers

top to bottom sometimes, never, always, sometimes

2 In your notebook, write about Nathan using adverbs of frequency.

Students write sentences in third person using present simple and adverbs of frequency describing the habits presented in Activity 1.

- Draw students' attention to the *Present Simple* box. Review the information in the chart, pointing out third-person –s and –es.

Answers

1. Nathan / He sometimes exercises. 2. Nathan / He never sleeps nine hours. 3. Nathan / He always eats healthy meals. 4. Nathan / He sometimes eats junk food.

3 Think Fast! **Write four sentences about you.**

Students do a thirty-second timed challenge: they personalize the grammar by writing sentences about their own habits.

Answers

Answers will vary.

Wrap-up

Students review adverbs of frequency with a game.

- Model the activity by saying some sentences about your routine, without saying the action. For example, *I usually do this at 6:30 in the morning.* Students guess: *You wake up!*
- Have students come to the front of the class and make similar sentences. The first student who guesses correctly is the next one to come up to the front.
- Continue as time allows or as long as students are engaged.

➡ **Workbook p. 143, Activities 1 and 2**

✔ **Homework Check!**

Workbook p. 143, Activities 1 and 2

Answers

1 Look and complete using *always, sometimes*
or *never.*

1. never, 2. sometimes, 3. always, 4. sometimes

2 Write about you.

Answers will vary.

Warm-up

Students review present simple.

- Write the adverbs *always, sometimes* and *never* on the board. Have each student make cards with the verb phrases from pages 70–73 on them.

- Students form groups of three or four and combine their cards. One member of the group deals the cards out, face down. Students take turns turning over a card and saying a sentence using the verb phrase and an adverb of frequency, for example, *I never exercise,* or *I usually wake up at 7:00.*

4 Look and number the dialogues. Then complete the dialogues.

Students number dialogues to put them in order according to the pictures. Then they complete the sentences with the correct present simple form of the verb in parentheses.

- Draw students' attention to the ***Present Simple, –** and ?* box. Read the information aloud. Elicit a few examples.

Answers

top to bottom, left to right exercises, 4, Does he sleep, 2, he does, 5, eats, 3, eats, 1

5 Think Fast! Unscramble the questions in your notebook. Then look and write the short answer.

Students do a three-minute timed challenge: they unscramble questions in present simple and write the positive or negative short answer to each.

- Draw students' attention to the ***Guess What!*** box. Read the information aloud.

Answers

1. Do you always have a healthy breakfast? No, I don't. 2. Do your parents go to the gym? Yes, they do. 3. Do we have P.E. in the afternoon? No, we don't. 4. Does your sister play basketball? No, she doesn't. 5. Does their school have a swimming pool? Yes, it does.

Extension

Students correct sentences in pairs.

- Provide a list of sentences with mistakes. Have students work in pairs to correct the mistakes.
    1. I wake up at 7:00 always.
    2. When you do study?
    3. Do he usually watch TV?
    4. You sometimes exercises.
    5. He always eating dinner at 6:00.
    6. We don't never eat junk food.
    7. Does you eat healthy meals?
    8. I sleeps eight hours.
- Liven things up by setting a stopwatch.

Answers

1. ~~7:00 always~~ I <u>always</u> wake up at 7:00. 2. ~~do you~~ When <u>do you</u> study? 3. ~~Do~~ <u>Does</u> he usually watch TV? 4. ~~exercises~~ You sometimes <u>exercise</u>. 5. ~~eating~~ He always <u>eats</u> dinner eat 6:00. 6. ~~don't~~ <u>We</u> <u>never</u> eat junk food. 7. ~~Does~~ <u>Do</u> you eat healthy meals? 8. ~~sleeps~~ I <u>sleep</u> eight hours.

Wrap-up

Students personalize Activity 5.

- Ask students to look at their unscrambled questions from Activity 5.

- Pairs take turns asking the questions and answering with information that's true for them. Monitor, offering help as needed.

➠ **Workbook pp. 143 and 144, Activities 3–6**

Reading & Listening

Objectives

Students will be able to read a timetable. They will also be able to think about questions other people will ask them.

Lesson 5   Student's Book pp. 74 and 75

✔ **Homework Check!**

Workbook pp. 143 and 144, Activities 3–6

Answers

3 Read and complete.

1. don't take, 2. don't do, 3. don't go, 4. doesn't eat, 5. doesn't go

4 Look and write the sentences.

1. I don't go to the gym on Mondays. 2. My friends play soccer after school. 3. Carol eats lunch at eleven o'clock. 4. You don't go to the gym in the evenings.

5 Complete and match.

1. go, No, they don't. 2. Does, Yes, she does. 3. Do, No, we don't. 4. have / eat, No, he doesn't.

6 Write the correct form of the verb. Then look and circle the correct option.

1. never, goes, 2. sometimes, watches, 3. always, does

 76

Warm-up

Students are exposed to the topic.

- Draw students' attention to the photos. Ask, *Do you like any of these activities? Do you know anyone who does them? Is there a Community Center near your house? What types of activities can you do there? What days do you go?*

- Allow students to express their thoughts. Don't focus too much on accuracy here.

1 Read the information in the website and circle the correct option.

Students read a schedule and use the information to answer questions about when classes are offered.

- Draw students' attention to the **Guess What!** box. Read the information aloud. Model the structure by saying the day and time of the yoga class: *Yoga is at 4:00 on Mondays. It's from 4:00-5:30.* Point out that you can say *four* instead of *four o'clock.*

Answers

1. c, 2. b, 3. c, 4. b, 5. b

2 Think Fast! Find a class for each person.

Students do a one-minute timed challenge: they analyze the information in the website and choose an activity for each person.

Answers

1. Guitar, 2. Keep Fit! for Seniors, 3. Photography, 4. Cooking

Wrap-up

Students find classes for each other.

- Students form pairs and tell each other times that they are free to take a class.

- Based on the times their partners are free, students take turns asking each other questions about their interests to find classes on the schedule to recommend to their partners. Tell students not to worry about the minimum age for each class for this activity.

- When pairs finish, take a poll to see the overall results of the class. How many students will take each class?

▶ **Workbook p. 145, Activity 1**

✔ **Homework Check!**

Workbook p. 145, Activity 1

Answers

1 Classify the activities.

Sports play soccer, play volleyball
Group Activities take dance classes, go out with friends, go to parties
Other play with my dog, read, watch TV, eat pizza

Warm-up

Students recall activities with a game.

- Play a game to help students recall the activities in the website: mime one of the activities, for example, yoga. The first student who guesses correctly comes to the front of the class and mimes another activity.

- Continue until all activities have been reviewed.

3 🎧²⁷ **Listen and complete the registration forms.**

Students listen for specific information and use it to complete forms.

- Draw students' attention to the **Be Strategic!** box. Read the information aloud and then draw their attention to the registration forms.

Answers

1. 15, Tai chi, Saturdays, 9:00 – 10:30, 2. 12, Guitar, Mondays and Wednesdays, 4:00 – 5:30, 3. 18, Photography, Friday, 7:00 – 8:30

Audio Script

RECEPTIONIST: Hi. This is Westgate Community Center. Can I help you?
CARLIE: Yes, I want to take a class.
RECEPTIONIST: OK. What's your name?
CARLIE: Carlie Smith.
RECEPTIONIST: How old are you?
CARLIE: 15.
RECEPTIONIST: Which class do you want to take?
CARLIE: Tai chi, please.
RECEPTIONIST: On Mondays and Thursdays?
CARLIE: No, on Saturdays, from 9:00 to 10:30.
RECEPTIONIST: Westgate Community Center. Can I help you?
JUSTIN: Yes, I want to take a class.
RECEPTIONIST: OK. What's your name?
JUSTIN: Justin. Justin Carter.
RECEPTIONIST: And how old are you, Justin?
JUSTIN: 12.
RECEPTIONIST: Which class do you want to take?
JUSTIN: Guitar, please.
RECEPTIONIST: On Mondays and Wednesdays?
JUSTIN: Yes, from 4:00 to 5:30.
RECEPTIONIST: OK. We'll see you on Monday at 4 o'clock, then!
RECEPTIONIST: Good afternoon. Westgate Community Center. Can I help you?
MICHELLE: Yes, I want to take a class.
RECEPTIONIST: OK. What's your name?
MICHELLE: Michelle Esposito.

RECEPTIONIST: And how old are you, Michelle?
MICHELLE: I'm 18.
RECEPTIONIST: Which class do you want to take?
MICHELLE: Photography, please.
RECEPTIONIST: On Friday, right?
MICHELLE: Yes, from 7:00 to 8:30.

4 **Choose a class for yourself.**

Students form small groups and choose classes they would like to take.

Answers

Answers will vary.

Stop and Think! Critical Thinking

How can an art or fitness class improve a person's health?

- Brainstorm with students words that have to do with physical and mental health. Write some on the board.

- Students form small groups to discuss the question *How can an art or fitness class improve a person's health?*

- Encourage students to reflect on how the classes offered at the community center can improve not just physical health, but also mental health.

Wrap-up

Students act out a role play.

- Have students form pairs. Using the registration forms and class schedule to guide their questions, students take turns role-playing the receptionist and the caller.

➤ **Workbook p. 145, Activities 2 and 3**

Preparing for the Next Lesson

Ask students to watch an introduction to Finnish culture: goo.gl/NvWiQh or invite them to look around on the website: goo.gl/XI35bq.

Culture

Lesson 7   Student's Book pp. 76 and 77

> ✔ **Homework Check!**
> Workbook p. 145, Activities 2 and 3
>
> **Answers**
> **2 Read about Rachel and Adrian. Write *R* (Rachel), *A* (Adrian), or *B* (Both).**
> 1. R, 2. B, 3. R, 4. B, 5. R
> **3 List three things you do in your free time.**
> Answers will vary.

Warm-up
Students discuss what they know to generate interest in a topic.

- Write *Finland* on the board. Ask students what they know about Finland.

- Ask students to make guesses about the following questions: 1. *Finland shares a border with which three countries? 2. What is the capital of Finland? 3. Some people call Finland "land of the midnight …" why? 4. What popular computer game was created in Finland?*

Answers

1. Sweden, Norway and Russia, 2. Helsinki, 3. There isn't much sunlight. 4. Angry Birds

1 Look at the map. Then read and circle the correct option.

Students use the map to choose the correct word to complete each sentence.

Answers

1. Europe, 2. cold, 3. small

2 Read and complete the table.

Students extract specific information from the text and use it to fill in the table.

Answers

Population 5.4 million, *Language* Finnish, Suomi, *Winter* -30°C, *Saunas* 2.2 million, *Foods* fish, potatoes, bread, cakes, reindeer meat, *Sports* ice hockey, pesapallo, skiing

3 🎧²⁸ Listen and match.

Students compare populations of countries.

Answers

China 1.4 billion, *The US* 300 million, *South Korea* 49.5 million, *New Zealand* 4.5 million, *Iceland* 330 thousand

Audio Script
Finland's population of 5.4 million is very small. Here are the populations of some other countries: China has a population of 1.4 billion people. In the US, there are 300 million people. South Korea has 49.5 million people. New Zealand has a population of 4.5 million people. Only 330 thousand people live in Iceland!

Wrap-up
Students reflect on what they've learned.

- Students think about and discuss in small groups how Finland compares to their country or countries considering these points: weather, population, sports, food, free time, animals and nature.

- Have the different groups report their opinions to the rest of the class.

▐▐▐➡ **(No homework today.)**

Warm-up

Students recall what they've previously learned.

- Set a stopwatch for one minute and have students list as much information as they can remember about Finland.

- If necessary, provide these categories: weather, nature, animals, population, language, sports, food and how people spend their time.

- Ask students to share their lists.

4 **Read and guess. Write *T* (True) or *F* (False) in the box.**
Students use previous information to make guesses.

Answers

Answers will vary.

5 **Listen and check. Then correct the false sentences.**
Students confirm their guesses and rewrite the false statements correctly.

Answers

1. F, Finland has 188,000 lakes. 2. T,
3. F, The national animal is the brown bear., 4. T

Audio Script

Finland has 188,000 lakes.
In the summer, the sun shines for 24 hours.
The national animal is the brown bear.
Finland is famous for its heavy metal music.

Extension

- If possible, bring in a selection of Finnish heavy metal music. Here are the names of some bands: Apocalyptica, Sonat Arctica, Sentenced and Nightwish. Be sure to listen to the music before class to make sure the lyrics are appropriate for your students.
- Play short tracks of the music and ask students what they think of it.

Stop and Think! Value

Why do you think saunas are popular in Finland?

- Ask students what they know about saunas. If necessary, explain that the word *sauna* is a Finnish word. (A sauna is a small room that's filled with hot air or steam. People sit in a sauna to relax and clean their bodies. After the heat of the sauna, people jump into an ice-cold bath or even snow! In public saunas, men and women have separate rooms. Ninety-nine percent of Finns take at least one sauna a week.)

- Ask *Why do you think saunas are popular in Finland?* Encourage students to recall the activities on the community center website, to get them thinking about health and reducing stress.

- Allow students to speak freely, without concentrating on accuracy.

Wrap-up

Students reflect on what they've learned.

- Draw students' attention to the text and the glossary. Have pairs discuss the following questions about Finland:
  Did you learn anything new about Finland?
  If so, what?
  What is one thing that surprised you?
  Would you like to travel to Finland?
  Why or why not?

▶ **(No homework today.)**

 Teaching Tip

Teaching Receptive Skills
When you're teaching receptive skills, be sure to provide enough exposure to listening and reading texts. Provide an appropriate task for the first time students read or listen. The task should be general in nature, for example, reading or listening for the main idea. The second time students read or listen, provide a task that focuses on more specific information, for example, reading or listening for details. If students need additional support, play the audio or allow the students to read the text several times. It might benefit the lesson to break up the listening or reading into small chunks.

Project

Lesson 9   Student's Book pp. 78 and 79

Warm-up

Students talk about their weekly activities to generate interest.

- Have pairs discuss the following questions:
  What activities do you do during the week?
  What activities do you do on the weekends?
  What do you think you spend the most time on: school, sports or other activities?

1 Circle the activities using the color code.

Students categorize vocabulary.

Answers

left to right, top to bottom blue, orange, orange, yellow, orange, yellow, orange, blue, orange, yellow, yellow

2 Look at Cheryl's routine on page 79. Then circle T (True) or F (False).

Students read an agenda for specific information.

Answers

1. T, 2. F (She goes to the gym on Sunday.), 3. T, 4. T, 5. F (Her favorite TV series is on Wednesdays at 8:30.), 6. T

Wrap-up

Students consolidate information.

- Draw students' attention to Cheryl's agenda. Model a sentence about an activity, for example, *Cheryl rides her bike from 4:30 to 6:00 on Tuesdays.*

- Students form pairs and make sentences about Cheryl's routine.

Warm-up

Students review routine activities.

- Students form small groups and brainstorm routine activities. Make it lively by setting a stopwatch for one minute.

- After one minute, have groups say their activities and write them on the board.

- Set the stopwatch for one more minute and have students categorize the activities into the groups *school, sports, friends and family, chores, other.*

- If students have not already done so, have them add these words and phrases to their vocabulary notebooks.

3 Make an agenda with your weekly routines.

Students create their own weekly agendas.

- Draw students' attention to the steps for making an agenda. Read them aloud or have a student read them.

- Point out the vocabulary and structures throughout the unit. Have students take out their vocabulary notebooks and provide dictionaries for reference.

- Students follow the first three steps to make their agendas. Encourage them to draw pictures as well as write the activities.

- When students have finished their agendas, they form pairs and talk about their weekly routines.

Answers

Answers will vary.

The Digital Touch

To incorporate digital media in the project, suggest one or more of the following:

- Make your agenda in Excel. Here's a site with instructions: goo.gl/CYvq1Y.
- Make your agenda online: goo.gl/C9AE.

Note that students should have the option to do a task on paper or digitally.

Wrap-up

Students talk about their classmates' agendas.

- Students form pairs and take turns telling their partners about another student's weekly routines.

- Come together as a class and ask students to compare their routines with their classmates'. How similar and different are their routines? Do any of them do the same activities?

➠ **Workbook p. 144, Activities 1 and 2 (Review)**

81

Review

Objective

Students will be able to consolidate their understanding of the vocabulary and grammar learned in the unit.

Lesson 11   Student's Book p. 80

> ✔ Homework Check!
>
> Workbook p. 144, Activities 1 and 2 (Review)
>
> **Answers**
> **1 Unscramble the routines.**
> 1. wake up, 2. do your homework, 3. brush my teeth,
> 4. eat dinner, 5. take a shower
> **2 Read and circle the correct option.**
> 1. don't, 2. go, 3. doesn't, 4. Does, 5. don't

Warm-up

Students list the vocabulary and grammar they have learned in the unit.

- Ask students to think of what they've learned in this unit.

- Elicit and list the grammar and vocabulary on the board. Vocabulary: Routines: *brush my teeth, do homework, get dressed, go to bed, go to school, eat breakfast / lunch / dinner take a shower, wake up*; Time: *six o'clock (six a.m. / p.m.), six (oh) five, a quarter past six, half past six (six thirty), a quarter to seven*. Grammar: present simple, adverbs of frequency (*always, sometimes, never*).

1 Read and match. Then look and number the photos.
Students match the beginnings of present simple sentences with their correct endings and match each sentence with the corresponding photo.

Answers

1. lunch at 1:30. 2. at 6:00 a.m. every day. 3. her teeth five times a day. 4. to school by bus. 5. a shower in the mornings?
left to right 4, 5, 3, 2, 1

2 Look and complete.
Students review routines vocabulary by completing phrases to match each photo.

Answers

1. eat / have, 2. get, 3. homework, 4. dinner

3 Look and circle the correct option.
Students choose the correct word to complete each time expression.

Answers

1. o', 2. past, 3. past, 4. to, 5. twenty-, 6. past

Wrap-up

Students review vocabulary.

- Have a treasure hunt with the student book.

- Write the following list of vocabulary phrases on the board or give pairs the list on paper: *brush my teeth, do homework, get dressed, go to bed, go to school, eat breakfast / lunch / dinner, take a shower, wake up*.

- Students form pairs to find either the vocabulary item or a picture showing it in the Student's Book. They write down the page or pages where the vocabulary is found.

- Set a stopwatch for three to five minutes, depending on your students and the time you have.

- Award one point for each vocabulary item or picture found, award one point for each additional time the vocabulary is found, award one additional point if the vocabulary is found outside of the unit and award an additional five points if all items are found. The pair with the most points when time is up wins.

▸ **(No homework today.)**

Warm-up

Students remember what they reviewed in the previous lesson.

- Ask students to say what they've reviewed. Elicit routines vocabulary, time and present simple statements.
- Ask students to say what they will be reviewing today. Elicit adverbs of frequency and present simple statements, questions and short answers.

4 **Look and circle *T* (True) or *F* (False).**

Students determine whether statements about the time people do activities are true or false based on the photos.

Answers

1. T, 2. F (Amy eats / has lunch at one o'clock.), 3. F (Tara wakes up at quarter to seven.), 4. F (Zack and Alex watch TV at a quarter past nine.)

5 **Write sentences using *never, sometimes* and *always*.**

Students write sentences with adverbs of frequency using cues.

Answers

1. They never eat breakfast. 2. My mom sometimes goes to the gym in the morning. 3. I sometimes watch TV after school. 4. My uncle sometimes plays tennis on Saturdays. 5. We never go to school by bus.

6 **Complete the sentences using the correct form of the verb.**

Students complete sentences with the correct present simple form of the verbs in parentheses. They also complete short negative and positive answers.

Answers

1. doesn't play, 2. Do, go, don't, 3. Does, wake up, does, 4. don't eat, 5. Do, watch, do

7 **Read and correct the sentences.**

Students rewrite sentences in present simple correctly.

Answers

1. ~~don't~~ Sam <u>doesn't</u> exercise a lot. 2. ~~play~~ Do you play basketball? Yes, I <u>do</u>. 3. ~~not~~ My friends <u>don't</u> go to the gym. 4. ~~eat~~ Natalia sometimes <u>eats</u> snacks. 5. ~~don't~~ Does he get up early? No, he <u>doesn't</u>. 6. ~~sports you~~ What sports <u>do</u> you play?

 Big Question

Students are given the opportunity to revisit the Big Question and reflect on it.

- Ask students to turn to the unit opener on page 69 and think about the discussion they had in the Warm-up in Lesson 1.
- Ask students to think of the other discussions they've had about routines. Ask them to take out their agenda and look it over.
- Students form small groups and discuss the following questions:
  » *How much time do you spend on schoolwork?*
  » *How much time do you spend on activities outside of school?*
  » *What do you think "work-life balance" means? Do you think you have a work-life balance? Explain.*

⭐ **Scorecard**

Hand out (and/or project) a *Scorecard*. Have students fill in their *Scorecards* for this unit.

▐▶ **Study for the unit test.**

<table>
<tr><th colspan="2">Grammar</th></tr>
</table>

Grammar

Frequency expressions: I surf the Internet <u>once a day</u>. / He checks his e-mail <u>twice a day</u>. / I make phone calls <u>twice a week</u>. / I make a video <u>three times a month</u>.

Question words: <u>What</u> do you watch? / <u>Who</u> do you call? / <u>Where</u> do you take photos? / <u>When</u> does she listen to music? / <u>How often</u> does he watch movies?

Vocabulary

Technology Collocations: check e-mail, listen to music, make phone calls, make a video, play games, send messages, share photos, shop online, surf the Internet, take photos, watch movies

E-mail: compose, delete, print, reply, save

Reading

Using key words

Writing

Writing search terms for a search engine

How important is technology to you?

In the first lesson, read the unit title aloud and have students look carefully at the unit cover. Encourage them to think about the message in the picture. At the end of the unit, students will discuss the big question: *How important is technology to you?*

Teaching Tip
Personalizing the Activities

Students, like all of us, like to talk about themselves. When you present new vocabulary and grammar, make sure students have the opportunity to use the new language to express their own opinions or experiences when the time comes for less-controlled, freer-speaking activities. This not only keeps students engaged, but it also helps them remember new language better if they have had the opportunity to use it in ways that are relevant to their own experience in some way.

85

Vocabulary

Objective

Students will be able to use **technology collocations** and **e-mail** vocabulary to talk about their use of technology.

Lesson 1 Student's Book p. 84

Warm-up

Students start thinking about the big question.

- Draw students' attention to the title of the unit. Read it aloud and ask *How important is technology to you?*
- Draw students' attention to the photos on page 83. In pairs, have students discuss what they see.
- Use this as an opportunity to diagnostically check what vocabulary and structures your students know.

1 🎧³⁰ Listen and number.

Students number the smartphone icons according to the order they hear them.

Answers

Watch movies 6, Play games 7, Shop online 8, Listen to music 5, Make a video 4, Check e-mail 2, Send messages 11, Make phone calls 10, Share photos 9, Surf the Internet 1, Take photos 3

Audio Script

AUNT: Hey, Maggie! Is that your new phone?
MAGGIE: Yes, it is!
UNCLE: It looks complicated!
MAGGIE: Well, yes, a little… But look. I have a lot of apps.
AUNT: Apps?
MAGGIE: Applications. I use this app to surf the Internet—like on a computer.
UNCLE: What's this…app…for?
MAGGIE: Oh, that's to check my e-mail.
AUNT: And what about this one?
MAGGIE: That's to take photos… and this one is to make a video.
UNCLE: Wow! And can you listen to music?
MAGGIE: Sure and I can watch movies, too.
AUNT: But isn't the screen a little small?
MAGGIE: Hmm, not really…
UNCLE: Is that a game?
MAGGIE: Yes, I play games on the bus. And I use this one to shop online.
AUNT: When do you use this app?
MAGGIE: I use it to share photos with my friends.
UNCLE: —But can you make phone calls?
MAGGIE: Yes, but I usually send messages.

---

2 🎧³⁰ Listen again and circle *T* (True) or *F* (False).

Students listen again for details and decide if a statement is true or false.

Answers

1. F (It is a little complicated, but she has lots of apps.), 2. T, 3. F (She says the screen is not really small.), 4. T, 5. F (She can make calls, although she usually sends text messages.)

3 Read and complete the sentences.

Students complete sentences with verbs.

Answers

1. surf, 2. make, send, 3. listens, watches, 4. share

4 Think Fast! Look and identify the functions of the devices. What can you do with them?

Students do a thirty-second timed challenge: they identify what devices shown in photos do.

Answers

left to right make phone calls, listen to music, watch movies, take photos, listen to music

Wrap-up

Students brainstorm devices.

- Draw students' attention to the phone in Exercise 4. Ask *What device do you use to make phone calls?*
- Have partners say what devices they use to listen to music, watch movies and take photos.

Extension

Play a game of telephone.

- Have students line up.
- The first student whispers a word or phrase from the lesson into the ear of the student next to him.
- That player then whispers the phrase to the following student in line.
- The game continues until it reaches the last student.
- Have the last player say the word or phrase aloud to see how much it has changed from the original.

▐▶ Workbook p. 146, Activities 1 and 2

Lesson 2   Student's Book p. 85

> ✔ **Homework Check!**
>
> Workbook p. 142, Activities 1 and 2
>
> **Answers**
> **1 Circle the verbs.**
> make, watch, share, listen, check, make, play, surf, shop, send
> **2 Look and label using some of the collocations in Activity 1.**
> 1. make a phone call, 2. take a photo, 3. check e-mail, 4. share photos, 5. shop online, 6. play games, 7. listen to music, 8. watch movies

Warm-up

Students review collocations and prepare for the content of the lesson.

- Have students make cards and write on them the verbs from the previous lesson: *check, listen, make, send, share, surf, watch.*

- In pairs, ask students to lay the cards facing down in a pile. Have them take turns drawing a card and holding it up. The other student should finish the collocation. Monitor, offering help as needed.

5 **Read and complete the e-mail.**

Students complete the text with verbs related to using e-mail.

Answers

save, reply, print, delete, compose

6 **Read and match.**

Students match words to make collocations.

Answers

1. important messages, 2. junk mail, 3. a new e-mail, 4. a paper copy, 5. to an e-mail

7 **Think Fast! Say the e-mail addresses.**

Students do a thirty-second timed challenge: they read e-mail addresses aloud.

- Draw students' attention to the **Guess What!** box. Read the information aloud and point to the corresponding parts of the e-mail address.

Wrap-up

Students practice writing e-mails.

- Have students exchange e-mail addresses and practice writing e-mails to each other using the e-mail as a model.

- Provide subjects to write about based on the units they've covered so far: a family party, describing a class or their classroom, their daily routine, etc.

➮ **Workbook p. 146, Activity 3**

 Teaching Tip

Conducting Writing Assignments

All of your students can write words in English, and most of them can write complete sentences. But writing a letter or paragraph is usually challenging. Here are some tips for in-class, and after-class, writing: Make sure the task is clear. Be sure to provide a model writing sample. Always provide an opportunity for students to finish outside of class. Be sure to give feedback, even if only collecting the writing and reading it, or having students meet to discuss what they wrote.

Grammar

Objective
Students will be able to use **frequency expressions** and **question words** to talk about their technology habits.

Lesson 3   Student's Book p. 86

> ✔ Homework Check!
>
> Workbook p. 146, Activity 3
>
> **Answers**
> **3 Read and complete the e-mail words.**
> 1. print, 2. reply, 3. compose, 4. save

Warm-up
Tell students to stand up and make a circle. Have them say and spell the days of the week, months of the year and seasons in order, forwards and backwards. Correct pronunciation and spelling.

1 Look and complete using a frequency expression.
Students complete sentences, based on a chart, using frequency expressions.
- Draw students' attention to the **Frequency Expressions** box. Read the information aloud. Elicit some examples of *every day, three times a week, twice a week* and *once a week*.

Answers
1. three times a week, 2. once a week, 3. every day, 4. twice a week, 5. three times a week

2 Write the frequency expressions on the chart.
Students put frequency expressions in order on the chart from *never* to *always*.

Answers
top to bottom, left to right twice a year, once a month, once a week, three times a week, every day, twice a day

3 🎧³¹ **Read the questions. Then listen and circle the correct option.**
Students answer questions about frequency based on a listening.

Answers
1. No, he doesn't. 2. No, he doesn't. 3. Yes, they do.

Audio Script
SOPHIE: Hi, James.
JAMES: Hi, Sophie.
SOPHIE: Can I ask you some questions? It's for my English class.
JAMES: Yeah, OK.
SOPHIE: Great! Thanks! Question 1. How often do you make phone calls?
JAMES: Hmm. I don't make phone calls every day. I make phone calls once or twice a week.
SOPHIE: OK. Do you listen to music every day?
JAMES: I don't have time. I listen to music once a week.
SOPHIE: Do your friends send you messages a lot?
JAMES: Yes, they text me every day.

4 Think Fast! In your notebook, write five sentences about your habits.
Students do a three-minute timed challenge: they write sentences expressing how often they use technology.

Answers
Answers will vary.

> ### Extension
> - Students play a game, Find Someone Who…
> - Provide students with prompts that begin with *Find someone who…*, for example, *has a smartphone, listens to music on her phone, doesn't have an e-mail account, doesn't play games on his phone, sends e-mails every day.*
> - Set a stopwatch for a few minutes. Have students stand up and ask and answer questions using the prompts. Have them write down their answers.
> - The winner is the student who has gotten the most positive answers at the end.

Wrap-up
Students make a chart showing their activities and how often they do them.
- Have students make a chart similar to the one in Activity 1 on page 86.
- Elicit the question from the listening *How often do you [make phone calls]?*
- Students form pairs and take turns asking and answering questions using their charts.

⟫ **Workbook p. 147, Activities 1-3**

88

✔ Homework Check!

Workbook page 147, Activities 1–3

Answers

1 Look and complete the sentences.

1. once a week, 2. twice a week, 3. every day,
4. three times a week

2 Write about Angie using frequency expressions.

1. Angie shops online once a month. 2. Angie takes selfies twice a week. 3. Angie surfs the Internet every day. 4. Angie listens to music twice a day. 5. Angie goes to school five times a week. 6. Angie shares photos twice a week.

3 In your notebook, answer about you.

Answers will vary.

Warm-up

Students review present simple questions with a game.

• Make a paper ball.

• Have students stand in a circle with their arms folded. Stand in the middle of the circle with the ball.

• Throw the ball to a student. If the student catches it, she throws it back to you and folds her arms again. If she doesn't catch it, she has to answer a question, for example, *Do you listen to music every day?*

• Repeats the procedure, tossing the ball back and forth until a student misses and asking questions.

• Continue playing as long as students are engaged.

5 Read and complete using the question words.

Students determine which question words complete each question correctly.

• Draw students' attention to the **Question Words** box. Read the question words aloud, pointing to the icons to confirm meaning.

• Draw students' attention to the **Guess What!** box. Read the information aloud and ask students to say which question word doesn't begin with a *Wh-*. (*How often?*)

Answers

Where, How often, What, When, Who

6 Unscramble and match.

Students unscramble words to write questions and match them with short answers.

Answers

1. What games do you have? FIFA 2016 and Mario Kart 8. 2. Where do you play volleyball? At school. 3. When do you watch movies? In the evenings. 4. Who do you take photos of? My friends and my mom.

7 Think Fast! Choose three questions. Ask and answer with a classmate.

Students do a five-minute timed challenge: they personalize the topic by asking and answering questions about themselves.

Answers

1. What time do you do your homework? 2. How often do you send messages? 3. What is your dad's name? 4. Where do you take photos? 5. What is your favorite food? 6. When do you play games?

Extension

Students play a game called Two Truths and a Lie.

• Students think of three statements about themselves: two are true, but one is a lie.

• Model the activity with statements about yourself. Students guess which statement is a lie.

• Have students form small groups of three or four and take turns telling each other their statements. They guess which is the lie.

• Come together as a class and have students share what they learned about each other.

Wrap-up

Students share what they learned about a classmate.

• Students meet with another classmate and tell each other what they learned about the classmates from Activity 7.

• Ask students to think about how similar or different they are from their classmates.

➜ **Workbook p. 148, Activities 4–6**

Reading & Writing

Objectives
Students will be able to use key words. They will also be able to write search terms for a search engine.

Lesson 5   Student's Book pp. 88 and 89

✔ **Homework Check!**

Workbook p. 147, Activities 4–6

Answers
4 Read and match.
1. Sports and movies. 2. My friends and family.
3. In the morning. 4. Twice a day.
5 Complete using the correct question word.
1. What, 2. Who, 3. Where, 4. How often
6 Read and complete using the correct forms of the verbs.
1. does, check, 2. does, take, 3. do, call, 4. does, send

Warm-up
Students write an acrostic poem to get them thinking about e-mailing.
- Write the letters E-M-A-I-L on the board, vertically.
- Ask students to think of technology words that begin with those letters.

- Model the first letter by writing a word, for example, *enter*. If necessary, show students the *enter* key on a computer keyboard.

1 Read and match the questions with the actions.
Students match information they might search for with a corresponding action.

Answers
1. find a definition, 2. find contact information,
3. find an address, 4. look up movie times, 5. look up facts

2 Read and complete the sentences.
Students read information about using search engines and then complete sentences.
- Draw students' attention to the **Be Strategic!** box. Read the information aloud and ask students to identify the key words in the searches. (technology, president, united states, math game algebra)

Answers
1. lowercase, 2. spelling, 3. punctuation, 4. key words, 5. quotation marks

Wrap-up
Students practice searching for information.
- Have pairs search for the same information on the three search engines, Google, Bing and Yahoo.
- Have the pairs meet with another pair and compare their findings.

➡ **Workbook p. 149, Activities 1 and 2**

✔ **Homework Check!**

Workbook p. 149, Activities 1 and 2

Answers

1 Read quickly and circle the correct option.
1. an app, 2. adults, 3. news articles
2 Read again and circle *T* (True) or *F* (False).
1. F (The app summarizes information in news articles.), 2. F (Each summary is a few sentences long.), 3. T, 4. T

Warm-up

Students think about how they use the Internet.
- Students work in small groups to list what types of information they search on the Internet.
- Students meet with members of other groups to share their lists.

3 Write search terms for each topic.

Students write search terms to search for information to answer the questions.

Answers

Answers will vary.

Extension

Students practice using search engines.
- Students form three groups. Have them search a topic, for example, cell phone use. One group searches only on Yahoo, one on Google and one on Bing.
- Have the groups share their findings with the class. Review the findings and explain what is reliable and what is not. Use this criteria:
- Is it from a site ending in .gov or .edu? Then it is probably reliable. If it is from a site ending in .com or .org, it may not be.
- Is there an author? If not, it may not be reliable.
- Is the information from within the past five years? If it's older, it may not be reliable.
- Help students go through the information, choosing reliable sources.

Stop and Think! Critical Thinking

How can you find reliable information on the Internet?
- Make sure students understand that the word *reliable* means *can be trusted to be true*.
- Tell students that reliable websites usually have the following:
  » the writer's name
  » a recent date (not older than five years)
  » an address ending in .gov or .edu

Wrap-up

Students compare search terms.
- Pairs compare their search terms in Activity 3.
- Have pairs go online and use the different search terms. Have them compare which terms are more successful.
- Encourage students to vary the order of the key words in the search terms to see what different information they get.

▮▮▶ **Workbook p. 149, Activities 3 and 4**

Preparing for the Next Lesson
Ask students to watch an introduction to Canada: goo.gl/QtJrgj or invite them to look around on the website: goo.gl/OG4wES.

Culture

Objectives

Students will be able to talk about Canada. They will also be able to talk about why it is important to learn about other people's cultures.

Lesson 7   Student's Book p. 90

✔ **Homework Check!**

Workbook p. 149, Activities 3 and 4

Answers

3 Read and mark (✓) the best summary of this article.

Nick D'Aloisi is the inventor of *Summly*, a successful phone and tablet app.

4 List your three favorite apps.

Answers will vary.

Warm-up

Students say what they know about Canada.

- Write *CANADA* on the board. Then write the headings from the Student's Book: *Name? Flag? Capital? Population? Famous Foods? Official Languages? Other Languages? Other Facts?*
- Ask students to say what they know about these topics. Write down any information they know to check after they've answered the questions in Activity 1.

1 Read and answer the questions.

Students answer questions based on facts about Canada.

Answers

1. village, 2. English and French, 3. a maple leaf,
4. French fries with cheese and gravy, 5. red,
6. FIFA / Prince of Persia / NBA Live

2 Read the descriptions. Who are the famous Canadians?

Students try to guess famous Canadians based on summaries of their achievements.

Extension

- Ask students to go online and do research on the famous Canadians in Activity 2 or other people.
- Ask them to say what key words they used in their searches.

Wrap-up

Students compare facts about Canada with facts about their country.

- Draw students' attention to the questions in Activity 1. Elicit similar questions about their country or countries, for example,
  » *Where does the name "[country]" come from? What does it mean?*
  » *What official language or languages does [country] have?*
  » *What does [country]'s flag look like?*
  » *What is a popular dish in [country]?*
  » *What color are the police uniforms in [country]?*
  » *What are some well-known people or things from [country]?*
- Pairs work together to answer the questions.
- Students share their answers with the class or in small groups.

➡ **(No homework today.)**

Warm-up

Students try to guess the cities in Canada.

- Write the cities listed in Activity 3 on the board: *Toronto, Vancouver, Montreal, Calgary, Iqaluit.*

- Set a stopwatch and have students mark the cities on the map.

- Tell them they will listen to check.

3 🎧³² Listen and number the cities.

Students listen to speakers talk about their cities and number the cities in the order they hear them.

Answers

left to right 1, 4, 5, 2, 3

Audio Script

SARINA JIANG: Hi, I'm from Vancouver, but my family is from China. You can play golf, go skiing and go kayaking in Vancouver—all on the same day.
AMARUK SATAA: Hello, my name is Amaruk Sataa and I am an Inuit. Amaruk means "Grey Wolf" in my language. I live in Iqaluit, the capital of Nunavut, in the north of Canada. It's very small. You can walk from the airport to downtown!
FLORENCE BOUCHARD: Salut! My name is Florence Bouchard and I live in the city of Montreal. French is my first language. In the winter, it is very cold, so we have many buildings underground, including banks, shopping malls and museums.
ALICE WILSON: Hey. I'm Alice Wilson and I live on a ranch near Calgary, Canada. Calgary is famous for rodeos. Yee haw!
AMIT SINGH: Hello. I'm Amit Singh and I live in Toronto. My family is originally from India. Here in Toronto, there are people from many different countries, especially Italians. Toronto has the biggest population of Italians outside of Italy.

3 🎧³² Listen again and match.

Students listen a second time and match the cities with specific information.

Answers

1. has a lot of Italian immigrants. 2. is good for golf. 3. has underground museums. 4. has ranches and rodeos. 5. is a very small town.

Stop and Think! Value

Are there people from different cultures in your country? What do you know about their cultures?

- Draw students' attention to the photos. Ask them to try to identify the people's culture. Elicit or provide the following: 1. Chinese, 2. Inuit, 3. French, 4. (most likely) European, 5. Indian

- Ask students if they have any of these cultures in their country. What other cultures are there?

Wrap-up

Students play Two Truths and a Lie about Canada.

- Say three new facts about Canada: two are true and one is a lie, for example, *Canada is the second largest country in the world. One-tenth (10%) of all the world's forests are in Canada. The coldest temperature ever recorded in Canada was -43 ºC (-45.5 ºF).* (Lie: The temperature was -63 ºC [-81.4 ºF]!)

- Pairs decide which is a lie. Then they discuss what new information they learned about Canada.

▶ **(No homework today.)**

🐝 Teaching Tip

Being Culturally Aware

Be sensitive when talking about other cultures in your classroom. Take time to make yourself more culturally aware. Familiarize yourself with terms used when talking about other cultures, for example, *multiculturalism, biculturalism, indigenous, cross-cultural.*

Project

Lesson 9   Student's Book pp. 92 and 93

Warm-up

Students play a miming game to generate interest.

- Take your phone and mime an activity you do with your phone, for example, play a game.

- The first student who guesses comes to the front of the class and mimes another activity. The student who guesses then comes up and mimes an activity.

- Continue as time permits or as long as students are engaged.

1 Read and mark (✔). Where do you use your phone to do these activities?

Students take a survey about the activities they do with their phones and where they do them.

Answers

Answers will vary.

2 Look at the technology infographic on page 93 and write the number.

Students study an infographic and find specific information to answer questions about it.

Answers

1. 3, 2. 43, 3. 41, 4. 5, 5. 29, 6. 32

Wrap-up

Students discuss the results of the survey.

- Draw students' attention to the survey in Activity 1.

- Elicit or provide the preposition for the types of transportation students mentioned in Activity 1: *in the car, on the train, in the bus / school bus, on foot.* Point out that in this case, we say *I listen to music while walking,* not ~~on foot~~. Also, point out that we use the definite article, *the,* with some forms of transportation in this case.

- Guide students in forming sentences to talk about the survey: *I watch videos on the train. I listen to music at home.*

- Students form pairs to talk about where they do these activities.

⫸ **(No homework today.)**

94

Warm-up

Students look at the infographic closely to prepare for the content of this lesson and generate interest.

- Have pairs discuss the following questions:
  1. *Where do most people listen to music? (on transportation) Is this true for you?*
  2. *What is the most popular activity at school? (send messages) Do you think this is OK?*
  3. *What do people do least at restaurants? (listen to music)*
  4. *What is the most popular activity at home? (play games) Is this true for you?*

- Ask students to report their findings to the rest of the class.

3 **Make a class technology infographic.**

Students make a class technology infographic based on survey results about how many times people do various technology activities in different places.

The Digital Touch

To incorporate digital media in the project, suggest one or more of the following:

- Use PowerPoint to make your infographic.
- Create your infographic in a template: goo.gl/xWUOiU.

Note that students should have the option to do a task on paper or digitally.

Wrap-up

Students display their infographics and give feedback.

- Have students display their infographics in the classroom.

- Students offer feedback and comments on their classmates' infographics. Provide some sentences for them to use, for example,

  » *I really like how you did this part!*

  » *The information in this part is very clear.*

  » *Where did you get this icon / picture? It works well!*

▥➡ **Workbook p. 148, Activity 1 (Review)**

Review

Objective

Students will be able to consolidate their understanding of the vocabulary and grammar learned in the unit.

Lesson 11   Student's Book p. 94

> ✔ **Homework Check!**
>
> Workbook p.148, Activity 1 (Review)
>
> **Answers**
>
> **1 Write and answer the questions.**
> 0. Answers will vary. 1. What's your favorite color? Answers will vary. 2. Where do you live? Answers will vary. 3. When do you go to bed? Answers will vary. 4. How often do you play sports? Answers will vary. 5. Who do you text? Answers will vary.

Warm-up

Students list the vocabulary and grammar they have learned in the unit.

- Ask students to think of what they've learned in this unit.

- Elicit and list the grammar and vocabulary on the board. Vocabulary: Technology collocations: *check e-mail, listen to music, make phone calls, make a video, play games, send messages, share photos, shop online, surf the Internet, take photos, watch movies*; e-mail: *compose, delete, print, reply, save*. Grammar: frequency expressions (*once / twice a day / week [three] times a month*); question words (*What? Who? Where? When? How often?*)

1 Read and match.

Students review collocations used in technology.

Answers

1. movies, 2. photos, 3. the Internet, 4. to music, 5. online, 6. phone calls, 7. e-mail, 8. messages

2 Find and correct the mistakes.

Students identify one mistake in the collocation in each sentence.

Answers

1. ~~makes~~ My sister always <u>takes</u> photos of her friends. 2. ~~the~~ Can I make <u>a</u> phone call? 3. ~~of~~ My friends listen <u>to</u> music on the bus. 4. ~~Internet~~ My parents don't shop <u>online</u>. 5. ~~surfs~~ Bill <u>plays</u> games on his computer. / ~~games~~ Bill surfs <u>the Internet</u> on his computer.

3 Find and circle five e-mail words. Then look and label the icons.

Students locate e-mail vocabulary in the puzzle and then write each next to the corresponding icon.

Answers

1. save, 2. reply, 3. compose, 4. delete, 5. print

4 Look, read and write the names.

Students study a chart and identify the person referred to in each sentence using information from the chart.

Answers

1. Vicky, 2. Max, 3. Vicky, 4. Vicky, 5. Zoe, 6. Zoe, 7. Vicky, Zoe

Wrap-up

Students personalize the vocabulary and grammar.

- Have pairs make cards with all the technology and e-mail collocations from this unit. Encourage them to use their vocabulary notebooks as reference.

- Pairs lay the cards on the desk. They take turns drawing a card and then asking and answering questions using the vocabulary item, for example, *How often do you text at school?*

- Monitor, offering help as needed. Make note of any mistakes in vocabulary or grammar for an anonymous feedback session after the activity.

➡ **(No homework today.)**

Warm-up

Students remember what they reviewed in the previous lesson.

- Ask students to say what they've reviewed. Elicit *technology collocations, e-mail vocabulary, frequency expressions.*
- Ask students to say what they will be reviewing today. Elicit *frequency expressions (word order)* and *question words.*

5   Unscramble and match.

Students practice word order of information questions by unscrambling sentences and matching them with short answers.

Answers

1. How often do you play video games? Twice a week. 2. What movies do your parents watch? Action movies. 3. Where does she do her homework? In the dining room. 4. Where do they take photos? At the park. 5. When do you send messages? In the evening.

6   Complete and answer the questions.

Students practice information questions and collocations and then provide their own short answers.

Answers

1. do, take, 2. are, 3. do, listen, 4. do, 5. do, check, Answers will vary.

7   Read the article and answer the questions.

Students read a text and about how often a boy uses technology and answer questions about the text using frequency expressions.

Answers

1. He sends messages every day. 2. He sends messages to his parents. 3. He plays games at an Internet café. 4. He watches basketball on TV. 5. He listens to music in the evenings.

 **Big Question**

Students are given the opportunity to revisit the Big Question and reflect on it.

- Ask students to turn to the unit opener on page 83 and think about the question "How important is technology to you?"
- Ask students to think about the discussions they've had about technology, the readings they've read and the infographic they made.
- Students form small groups to discuss the following:
  - » *How important is technology to you?*
  - » *Do you think you spend too much time using technological devices? Why or why not?*
  - » *Do you think a person can become addicted to, or can't live without, technology? Explain.*

⭐ Scorecard

Hand out (and/or project) a *Scorecard*. Have students fill in their *Scorecards* for this unit.

➡ **Study for the unit test.**

7 What are you wearing?

Grammar
Present continuous: Kyle <u>is wearing</u> a T-shirt. He<u>'s not wearing</u> a coat. <u>Are</u> you <u>wearing</u> a new blouse?

Vocabulary
Clothing: blouse, boots, coat, dress, hat, jacket, jeans, pajamas, pants, sandals, scarf (scarves), shoes, shorts, skirt, socks, sweater, tie, T-shirt
Adjectives: casual, cheap, comfortable, elegant, expensive, popular, useful
Prices

Listening
Listening for detail

Writing
Using adjectives

What are you wearing?

In the first lesson, read the unit title aloud and have students look carefully at the unit cover. Encourage them to think about the message in the picture. At the end of the unit, students will discuss the big question: *What are you wearing?*

Teaching Tip

Using Role Plays in the Classroom

A role play is any speaking activity where you act, taking on the role of another person in an imaginary situation. Using role plays in your classroom adds variety, changes the pace and provides opportunities for maximum language production. To ensure a role play is successful, make sure you prepare your students. Anticipate what their language needs might be and supplement the target language accordingly. Students may need the extra support of having the language on the board. Finally, bring the situations to life when possible. Something as simple as writing *Benchmark Clothing Shop* on the board when students are role-playing a salesperson and customer can set the mood and make the activity more memorable and fun.

 **Vocabulary**

Objective
Students will be able to use **clothing**, **adjectives** and **prices** vocabulary to talk about fashion.

Lesson 1   Student's Book p. 98

Warm-up
Students start thinking about the Big Question.
- Draw students' attention to the title of the unit. Read it aloud and ask *What are you wearing?*
- Draw students' attention to the photo. Ask *Where is this?* Elicit or provide *In a (clothing) store / mall.* Draw students' attention to the clothes in the photo. Ask *Do you like the clothes?* Elicit answers, but don't worry about accuracy.
- In pairs, have students discuss what they see.
- Use this as an opportunity to diagnostically check what vocabulary and structures your students know.

1 Read the blog and find the clothing items in the webpage of the week.
Students identify clothing vocabulary in a text, matching the vocabulary with photos.

2 Read and circle *T* (True) or *F* (False).
Students identify true and false statements based on a reading.

 100

Answers
1. F (Sandals or pumps go with a formal dress.),
2. F (Blouses are for girls.), 3. T, 4. F (T-shirts are casual.)

3 Think Fast! In your notebook, write five items you have in your closet.
Students do a two-minute timed challenge: they personalize the vocabulary by listing clothing items in their own closets.

Answers
Answers will vary.

Wrap-up
Students make a clothing store directory.
- Draw students' attention to the picture on page 97. Ask *What clothes can you see in the shop?* Pairs tell each other the clothing items. *(scarf, coat, jacket, sweater, shirt, jeans)*
- Have pairs make a clothing store directory. Students organize the clothes into groups. Elicit and provide groups, for example, *casual wear, formal wear, men's wear, women's wear, shoes, outdoor wear, seasonal.* Have each student make the directory in his or her vocabulary notebook.
- Students form new pairs and say what they have in their departments: *We have wool scarves and hats in many colors in our outdoor wear.*

 Workbook p. 150, Activities 1 and 2

Teaching Tip
Assessing Students Informally
Find opportunities to diagnostically assess your students. These will usually be production-oriented activities, such as speaking or writing exercises. While it's good to review known language, it's only effective when the amount of time spent on it is appropriate and it's useful for your students. If your students already know some vocabulary or structures, modify your lesson to reflect that.

✔ **Homework Check!**

Workbook p. 150, Activities 1 and 2

Answers

1 Look and label.

$14 scarf, *$18* tie, *$21.29* blouse, *$19.99* skirt, *$32* boots, *$35* sweater, *$55* jacket, *$17.50* hat, *$12* T-shirt, *$59.79* pants, *$125* coat, *$89.99* dress

2 Read, find and write the questions.

1. How much are the pajamas? 2. How much is the coat? 3. How much are the pants? 4. How much is the T-shirt?

Warm-up

Students race to identify the person in the photos.

- Students form small groups and line up at the board.

- Tell students to look at the photos on page 98. Have students label the people in the photos, starting on the top row on the left, A, B, C, D, E and F (skipping the photos of the coat and the shoes).

- Tell students that you will describe a person, and a member of each group will write the corresponding letter on the board for their group. The group that correctly identifies each person first gets a point, and the group with the most points wins.

- You can use these descriptions: *1. I'm wearing jeans and a yellow jacket. 2. I'm wearing a shirt and a tie. 3. I'm wearing pumps and a dress. 4. I'm wearing boots and a skirt. 5. I'm wearing a T-shirt and jeans. 6. I'm wearing a sweater and a scarf.*

Answers

1. D, 2. F, 3. C, 4. E, 5. B, 6. A

4 Look and mark (✓) the item that doesn't belong.

Students choose the clothing that doesn't fit in each category.

Answers

left to right 3rd (pumps), 2nd (flip flops), 1st (old boots), 2nd (tie)

5 Read and circle the correct definition.

Students determine the definitions of the clothing adjectives based on the pictures in Activity 4.

Answers

1. informal, 2. sophisticated, 3. doesn't cost a lot, 4. not cheap

6 In your notebook, describe what they are wearing.

Students describe the clothes the people in the photographs are wearing.

Answers

Answers will vary; examples: *Man* pants, a jacket, brown shoes and a scarf. *Woman* a black skirt, a black jacket, a white blouse and sunglasses.

Extension

- Play a game, Expanding Sentence, to teach students adjective order. Play with the entire class or bigger groups of five or six.

- Write this phrase on the board: *two smelly cheap big old brown leather cowboy boots*. Explain that this is the order of adjectives in English: number, opinion, quality, size, age, color, material, purpose.

- Write a sentence on the board, for example, *The girl has a scarf*.

- Have the first student add an adjective to the noun, saying the sentence aloud, for example, *The girl has a green scarf*.

- The next student adds another adjective, for example, *The girl has a warm green scarf*.

- The next student adds another adjective, and the game continues until all students have added an adjective to the sentence.

Wrap-up

Students use adjectives in a role-play.

- Tell students they will go shopping. They will be a customer and a sales assistant.

- Provide a sample dialogue:
  » SALESPERSON: *I really [that jacket]! It looks good on you.*
  CUSTOMER: *Thanks! How much is it?*
  S: *It's [$75].*
  C: *That's too [expensive].*
  S: *Well, how about this one? It's [$50].*
  C: *OK. I'll try it on.*

- Have students practice using other clothing items, prices and adjectives.

▶ Workbook p. 151, Activities 3 and 4

 Teaching Tip

Expanding Activities

Give students the chance to show what they know. When you can, expand an activity. Students have a lot to contribute from their own bank of knowledge and experience. There are many benefits to allowing for this in your classroom: quieter students often contribute more when they can choose, and students are more engaged when the activity has personal context for them.

Grammar

Objective

Students will be able to use the **present continuous** to talk about ongoing actions in the present.

Lesson 3   Student's Book pp. 100 and 101

> ✔ **Homework Check!**
>
> Workbook p. 151, Activities 3 and 4
>
> **Answers**
>
> **3 Complete the sentences with the correct adjectives.**
> 1. comfortable, 2. elegant, 3. cheap, 4. casual, 5. expensive, 6. popular, 7. useful
>
> **4 Unscramble the sentences.**
> 1. Henry has an expensive jacket. 2. This is a comfortable T-shirt. 3. Ugg boots are very popular. 4. A coat is useful in the winter.

Warm-up

Students play a memory game.

- Set a stopwatch for ten seconds. Tell pairs to look at each other and try to remember each other's clothes.

- Have students turn their backs to each other. They tell their partner the clothes he or she has on.

- When students have finished, they turn around and check to see how much they could remember.

1 **Look and mark (✓) the activities in the comic.**

Students identify activities shown in a comic.

Answers

dancing, eating, listening to music, studying, texting, taking photos

2 🎧³³ **Listen and number the scenes.**

Students put the frames of the comic in order by numbering them based on the listening.

Answers

left to right, top to bottom 5, 4, 1, 3, 2

Audio Script

1. TRISHA: Hello?
   ROSE: Hi, Trisha! It's Rose.
   TRISHA: Hi, Rose. Where are you?
   ROSE: I'm at the Middle School 60s party. It's great!
2. TRISHA: Cool!
   ROSE: Yeah. Melissa and Thomas are dancing. Oh, and Anthony's here, too.
3. TRISHA: Is he dancing?
   ROSE: No, he isn't. He's taking photos for the school newspaper.
4. ROSE: …And Lilly and Paul are here.
   TRISHA: What are they doing?
   ROSE: Lilly's texting… She looks worried. Paul is eating…as always!
5. ROSE: Can't you come to the party?
   TRISHA: No, I can't. I'm studying for a big math exam.

3 🎧³³ **Listen again and label the characters in the comic.**

Students identify characters shown in the comic based on a listening.

Answers

left to right, top to bottom Trisha, Paul, Lilly, Rose, Anthony, Melissa, Thomas

4 **Think Fast!** **Look and write the names.**

Students do a two-minute timed challenge: they identify characters in the comic based on descriptions.

Answers

1. Paul, 2. Lilly, 3. Trisha, 4. Anthony, 5. Melissa

Wrap-up

Students retell the story in the comic.

- Draw students' attention to the comic strip.

- Have pairs retell the story, using the comic scenes as prompts.

➤ **Workbook p. 151, Activities 1 and 2**

> ✔ **Homework Check!**
>
> Workbook p. 151, Activities 1 and 2
>
> **Answers**
>
> **1 Read and mark (✓) the correct description.**
> 1st
> **2 Read and complete using the correct forms of the verbs.**
> 1. are eating / 're eating, 2. am studying / 'm studying, 3. is watching, 4. are taking, 5. is singing

Warm-up

Students play charades to practice the present participles.

- Model the game by acting out one of the activities from Activity 1, for example, taking photos. Ask *What am I doing?* Elicit *Taking photos.*

- Have volunteer students come to the front of the class, acting out the different activities as the rest of the class guesses.

5 **Read and complete the chart.**

Students complete a chart showing how the present continuous is formed.

- Draw students' attention to the **Present Continuous** box. Point out that the present continuous is formed with the verb *be*.

- Draw students' attention to the **Guess What!** box. Read the information aloud and draw students' attention to the participles in Activity 1 on page 100. Ask students to find examples of verbs with spelling changes like *dance*. (*skate* ➔ *skating, take* ➔ *taking*) Provide students with other examples of verbs with spelling changes like *sit*. (*swim* ➔ *swimming, stop* ➔ *stopping, run* ➔ *running*)

Answers

top to bottom re, ing, are

6 **Read and circle the correct option.**

Students identify the correct form of *be* to complete sentences in present continuous.

Answers

1. is, 2. aren't, 3. are, 4. Are, 5. Is, 6. 'm

7 **Think Fast!** **In your notebook, write sentences using the cues.**

Students do a two-minute timed challenge: they write sentences in present continuous using cues.

Answers

1. I am not studying. 2. We are dancing. 3. She is wearing a blue dress. 4. They are not wearing boots. 5. Are you doing homework? 6. Are they exercising?

Wrap-up

Students play a game using the present continuous.

- Play the memory game from the Warm-up in Lesson 3, but have students form different pairs. This time, they say what their partner is wearing: *She is wearing a green…*

▐▐▐▶ Workbook p. 152, Activities 3 and 4

Listening & Writing

Objectives

Students will be able to listen for detail. They will also be able to use adjectives in their writing.

Lesson 5   Student's Book pp. 102 and 103

> ✔ **Homework Check!**
>
> Workbook p. 152, Activities 3 and 4
>
> **Answers**
>
> **3 Read and number the lines of the dialogue.**
> *1, 4, 7, 8, 5, 6, 3, 2*
> **4 Write questions using the cues. Then number the answers below.**
> 1. Are they doing homework? 2. What are you listening to? 3. When are we having lunch?
> 4. Who are you talking to? 5. Where are we going?
> *left to right, top to bottom* 1, 2, 3, 4, 5

Warm-up

Students predict what a listening will be about.
- Draw students' attention to the photos. Ask *Where are they?* Let students express themselves.
- Ask *What are they doing?* Elicit answers.

1 Look at the photos and number the places.
Students number phrases to match them with the photos of the places.

Answer

left to right, top to bottom 5, 4, 2, 1, 3

2 🎧³⁴ **Listen and write the photo captions.**
Students write captions for photos based on the listening.
- Draw students' attention to the *Be Strategic!* box. Read the information aloud and encourage students to use adjectives in their captions.

Answers

Answers will vary; examples: 1. Going to the mall, 2. Buying expensive shoes, 3. Watching a horror movie, 4. Having a delicious lunch, 5. Playing video games

Audio Script

Mom: Are you back already?
Jo: Yeah. But what a great day! Look at my photos!
Jo: This is us on the bus. We're going to the mall.
Mom: Oh, look. I love that store. What is Elsie buying?
Jo: Elsie's buying expensive shoes.
Jo: And here we are at the movie theater. We're watching a horror movie!
Mom: Oh, that's scary!
Jo: And here we're having delicious lunch!
Mom: Mmm. Chinese food.
Jo: In this photo, we're playing video games. Elsie's very good at them.

3 🎧³⁴ **Listen again and complete.**
Students listen for details and use them to complete the sentences.

Answers

1. Are you, 2. at my, 3. that's, 4. this photo

Stop and Think! Critical Thinking

What do you share online? What is good to share? What isn't?
- Ask students if they think the photos Jo posted online are OK to share. Why or why not?
- Ask students to think about the photos they have on their phones. What kinds of photos do they post online? What kinds of photos are OK to share? Why?

Wrap-up

Pairs role-play characters from a listening.
- Tell pairs to image that one of them is Elsie and the other is her mom or dad.
- Draw their attention to the photos and play the recording again if necessary.
- Pairs role-play a new conversation, similar to the listening, between Elsie and her mom or dad.

➡ **Workbook p. 153, Activities 1 and 2**

Lesson 6 — Student's Book pp. 102 and 103

✔ **Homework Check!**

Workbook p. 153, Activities 1 and 2

Answers
1 Look and label.
jacket, shirt, skirt
2 What do these clothes have in common?
Read and check your ideas.
They are all made of denim.

Warm-up

Students identify adjectives in a text.

- Set a stopwatch for one minute.

- Draw students' attention to the blog on page 98. Have pairs race against the clock to find as many descriptive adjectives as they can. The adjectives listed here are the ones your students are most likely to identify: *casual, comfy, elegant, formal, family, special, black, gray, navy, black, brown, expensive, cheap, essential, cool, useful, good, warm.*

- The pair with the most adjectives when time is up are the winners.

◁ Read and underline the adjectives.

Students identify adjectives in sentences.

Answers
1. great, 2. hard, 3. delicious, 4. funny, 5. interesting

5 Write sentences using the present continuous.

Students use cues to write sentences in the present continuous.

Answers
1. We are eating some delicious pasta. 2. I am making a long scarf. 3. He is reading a great book. 4. They are watching a popular TV series.

6 Think Fast! Describe the pictures using adjectives.

Students do a one-minute timed challenge: they describe pictures using adjectives.

Answers
Answers will vary; examples: 1. fun, 2. hard, 3. delicious, 4. scary

Wrap-up

Pairs imagine what a person in their life is doing at the moment.

- Model the activity by saying what you think someone close to you is doing: *I wonder what my brother is doing right now? Hmm… He's at work. It's 11:30. I think he's getting ready to go to lunch. He's finishing writing some e-mails.*

- Pairs say what someone in their lives is doing at that moment.

▮▮▶ Workbook p. 153, Activities 3 and 4

Preparing for the Next Lesson
Ask students to watch an introduction to Vietnam: goo.gl/icJCHd.

 *Culture*

Objectives

Students will be able to talk about Vietnam. They will also be able to talk about why a lot of clothing is manufactured in countries like Vietnam.

Lesson 7   Student's Book pp. 104 and 105

✔ **Homework Check!**

Workbook p. 153, Activities 3 and 4

Answers

3 Read and match.

1. produced denim jeans for miners. 2. it is durable. 3. all over the world. 4. denim its blue color. 5. also produce jeans.

4 What clothing items does your family have? Make a list in your notebook.

Answers will vary.

Warm-up

Students identify clothing items.

- Students form pairs and make a list of all of the clothing items they can see on pages 104 and 105.

- Have pairs share their answers with the class. The pairs that correctly identify the most items win. Pairs that use adjectives to describe the clothing get bonus points.

 106

1 Read and circle the correct option.

Students choose words to correctly complete facts about Vietnam based on a reading.

Answer

1. a, 2. c, 3. a, 4. a, 5. c, 6. a

2 Read and match.

Students match the beginnings of sentences with their correct endings to learn more facts about Vietnam.

Answers

1. transportation, travel and work. 2. friendly and intelligent. 3. town in Vietnam. 4. Racing Festival. 5. before the race. 6. in each race. 7. kilometers long. 8. swim and play soccer.

3 🎧³⁵ Listen and check.

Students listen to check the sentences they formed in the previous activity.

Audio Script

In Asia, people use elephants for transportation, travel and work. Asian elephants are friendly and intelligent. In the town of Tay Nguyen in Vietnam, there is an Elephant Racing Festival every year. Before the race, the elephants have special food. There are ten elephants in each race. Races can be one or two kilometers long. After the races, the elephants also take part in a swimming competition and a soccer game.

Wrap-up

Students express their opinions on information in a listening.

- Have pairs or groups of three discuss the following questions: Do you think elephants should be used for transportation and work? Should they be used in races? Why or why not?

▐▌▌➡ **(No homework today.)**

Warm-up

Students discuss what they know about clothing factories to generate interest.

- Have students check the labels on their clothing and shoes. Ask them to identify the country where the clothes and shoes were made.

- Have students find the countries on a map. Ask *What part of the world are most of the countries in?* Elicit or provide *Southeast Asia*.

◄ 🎧³⁶ **Listen and circle *T* (True) or *F* (False).**

Students listen to the second part of the recording and determine whether statements are true or false.

Answers

1. T, 2. F (Workers don't earn a lot of money.), 3. F (More than 50% of the workers didn't complete secondary school.), 4. T, 5. T

Audio Script

The clothing industry is very important in Vietnam. Many companies like Zara, Columbia, Forever21, Levi, and Nike make clothing and shoes there. A typical clothing factory worker works from seven o'clock in the morning until five o'clock in the afternoon. Most Vietnamese factory workers earn $50 to $100 a month. Vietnam is so famous for its clothing that some people travel there just to go shopping! Clothing from Vietnam is popular in the US, Europe and Japan. The US buys more Vietnamese clothing than any other country.

Stop and Think! Value

Do you know where your clothing comes from? Why do you think famous brands use factories there?

- Tell students to imagine that they are starting a clothing company. Ask *How does a clothing company make money? If you buy a shirt for $15, how much money does the company make?* Elicit that the company makes the price minus the cost of producing the shirt.

- Ask *Why does it cost different amounts to make clothing in different countries?* Elicit or provide *The people who make the clothes earn more money in some countries than in others.*

- Tell students to discuss in small groups why they think countries like Vietnam and China manufacture so much clothing.

Wrap-up

Students express opinions on a listening.

- Have small groups discuss the following questions:
  - » Do you have any clothes made in Vietnam?
  - » Do you think the amount of money clothing industry workers make is fair?
  - » What do you think you can do to change the situation in clothing factories?

▐▐▐➡ **(No homework today.)**

107 ◄

Project

Lesson 9   Student's Book p. 106

Warm-up

Students play a game to generate interest and review vocabulary.

- Explain that students will either "be" a color, an adjective, a piece of clothing or a relationship.

- To assign their categories, have students go around the room, each saying one of these words, in this order: *Color. Adjective. Clothing. Relationship.*

- Say a word that is a color, an adjective, a piece of clothing or a relationship, for example, *navy*. The students who are colors must stand up quickly. If a student doesn't stand up, he is out of the game.

- The students then sit down and you say another word, for example, *best friend*. The students who are relationships stand up.

- Continue as time permits or as long as students are engaged.

1 Classify the words.

Students classify words into categories.

108

Answers

Colors green, blue, white, red, black
Adjectives comfortable, casual, elegant, useful, cool
Clothes skirt, shirt, hat, shoes, shorts
Relationships friend, dad, brother, grandma, sister

2 Complete the descriptions.

Students write descriptions of people's clothes.

Answers

Boy jeans, a gray jacket, a white T-shirt, black sneakers and a backpack, *Girl* a black skirt, a white sweater, a brown hat, boots

Wrap-up

Students play a guessing game.

- Pairs take turns describing what a classmate is wearing without saying the classmate's name: *She is wearing a blue shirt, jeans, black shoes and a gray scarf.* The other student guesses who is being described.

▸ **(No homework today.)**

Warm-up

Students think of VIPs in their lives to prepare for the project.

- Draw students' attention to the Relationships column in the chart in Activity 1.

- Have students think about their grandmas, sisters, brothers, dads and friends. Ask them to think of other people who are important in their lives.

- Pairs tell each other about two or three VIPs in their lives.

3 **Make VIP (Very Important Person) Profiles for four or more people.**

Students make profiles of people in their lives.

- Draw students' attention to the steps.

- Encourage them to make notes and draft the information before finalizing their profiles.

> **The Digital Touch**
>
> To incorporate digital media in the project, suggest one or more of the following:
> - Make a collage of your photos and captions: goo.gl/XFOscZ.
> - Make a video of the people in your VIP profile to send to them on your phone.
>
> Note that students should have the option to do a task on paper or digitally.

Wrap-up

Students talk about the people in their profiles.

- Display the profiles in your classroom.

- Invite students to "introduce" the people to their classmates.

- Encourage students to ask each other questions about the people.

➡ **Workbook p. 152, Activity 1 (Review)**

Review

Objective

Students will be able to consolidate their understanding of the vocabulary and grammar learned in the unit.

Lesson 11   Student's Book p. 108

✔ **Homework Check!**

Workbook page 152, Activity 1 (Review)

Answers

1 Read and correct the mistakes.

1. ~~is~~ are, 2. ~~pijamas~~ pajamas, 3. ~~espensive~~ expensive 4. ~~He wearing~~ He is wearing

Warm-up

Students list the vocabulary and grammar they have learned in the unit.

- Ask students to think of what they've learned in this unit.
- Elicit and list the grammar and vocabulary on the board. Vocabulary: clothing: *blouse, boots, coat, dress, hat, jacket, pajamas, pants, scarf, scarves, skirt, socks, sweater, tie, T-shirt*; adjectives: *casual, cheap, comfortable, elegant, expensive, formal, popular, useful*. Grammar: *present continuous*.

1 Look and circle the correct option.

Students identify clothing and accessories.

Answers

1. blouse, 2. hat, 3. sandals, 4. boots, 5. scarf, 6. skirt, 7. pajamas, 8. sweater, 9. coat

2 Classify the clothing items.

Students group clothing items according to whether they take the singular or plural form of a verb.

Answers

How much is the... dress, hat, scarf, tie
How much are the... jeans, pants, shoes, shorts

3 Look and complete the prices.

Students write out prices in words.

- Read the first price aloud: *Sixty-eight dollars*. Then read the second one: *Sixteen twenty-five*. Point out that when a price has cents, we don't usually say *dollars*.

Answers

1. sixty-eight, 2. twenty-five, 3. five, nine, 4. ninety-five, 5. fifty-six

4 Unscramble the adjectives.

Students unscramble letters and write the adjectives.

Answers

1. casual, 2. comfortable, 3. elegant, 4. expensive, 5. cheap, 6. useful

Extension

Explain the concept of collective nouns.

- Draw students' attention to the photos on pages 98 and 99. Ask students to find the plural items. Elicit *shoes, pumps, flip-flops, boots*.
- Point to the photo of the man in Activity 6. Point to his pants and ask *Are they singular or plural?* Let students think about this a little. Explain that some pieces of clothing are what's called *collective nouns*. They are one item, but take a plural verb. They cannot be written without the *–s*. We would not say *pant*. Collective nouns are often used with the phrase *a pair of*.
- Ask students to name other clothing that are collective nouns and practice using *a pair of* with them: *a pair of pants, jeans, pajamas. stockings, tights*.
- Tell students not to be confused with true plural nouns, for example, *socks, gloves, boots, slippers, shoes* and *sandals—one sock, two socks*. You can use *a pair of* with these words as well.
- Point out that students use a plural verb with collective and plural nouns: *How much are the jeans?*

Wrap-up

Students role-play a salesperson and a customer.

- Have students decide on prices for the clothes on page 108. Guide them with writing dollars and cents.
- Pairs role-play a salesperson and customer. The customer asks the prices of items and the salesperson answers. Encourage students to use other language from the role play in Lesson 2.

➠ **(No homework today.)**

Warm-up

Students remember what they reviewed in the previous lesson.

- Ask students to say what they've reviewed. Elicit *clothing vocabulary and adjectives.*
- Ask students to say what they will be reviewing today. Elicit *present continuous.*

5 Read and complete using *is* or *are*.

Students complete sentences with the correct forms of *be.*

Answers

1. is, 2. are, 3. are, 4. is, 5. is

6 Complete the sentences using the present continuous.

Students complete sentences with the present continuous forms of the verbs in parentheses.

Answers

1. is studying, 2. is not wearing, 3. are taking, 4. am not studying, 5. are listening to, 6. is watching

7 Unscramble and match.

Students unscramble questions and match them to the correct answers.

Answers

1. What are your friends doing? Playing soccer.
2. Is he watching a scary movie? No, he isn't.
3. How are you doing? I'm fine, thanks. 4. Is Fiona wearing a new coat? Yes, she is. 5. Who is she texting? Her mom.

8 What are they wearing? Look and describe using colors and adjectives.

Students describe what a boy and girl are wearing in two photos.

Answers

Answers will vary.

 **Big Question**

Students are given the opportunity to revisit the Big Question and reflect on it.

- Ask students to turn to the unit opener on page 97 and think about the question "What are you wearing?"
- Ask students to think about the discussions they've had about clothing, the texts they've read and the profiles they made.
- Students form small groups to discuss the following:
  » *Do you often buy new clothes? Do you ever buy "second-hand" clothes?*
  » *Do you think it's important to dress properly for different occasions? Explain.*
  » *There's an expression "Clothes make the person." What do you think that means? Do you agree? Why or why not?*

 Scorecard

Hand out (and/or project) a *Scorecard*. Have students fill in their *Scorecards* for this unit.

➠ **Study for the unit test.**

8   *What do you love doing?*

Grammar
Likes and dislikes: My friends <u>like</u> watching TV. I <u>love</u> going shopping. My brother <u>hates</u> doing chores.   ***Let's:*** <u>Let's</u> watch a movie.

Vocabulary
Vacation Activities: cook, get a tan, go climbing, go shopping, go snorkeling, go surfing, go swimming, go waterskiing, lift weights, play miniature golf

Listening
Listening for large numbers

Reading
Identifying similarities and differences

? What do you love doing?

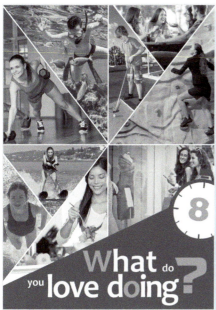

In the first lesson, read the unit title aloud and have students look carefully at the unit cover. Encourage them to think about the message in the picture. At the end of the unit, students will discuss the big question: *What do you love doing?*

Teaching Tip

Teaching Vocabulary

When teaching vocabulary, point out patterns. Ask students to find them in texts, for example, *go swimming* and *go climbing* on page 112 (*go + -ing* form). After students have read a text or listened to a recording, have them choose three phrases, rather than words, they'd like to learn. Students can pick up expressions, collocations and idioms more easily this way. When teaching vocabulary, ask students if there is anything they'd like to learn for active use. This puts the focus on the student, rather than always on the target language. Be sure to point out high-frequency items in vocabulary sets, and remind students to enter new vocabulary into their vocabulary notebooks.

Vocabulary

Objective

Students will be able to use **vacation activities** vocabulary to talk about things they love to do.

Lesson 1 Student's Book pp. 112 and 113

Warm-up

Students start thinking about the Big Question.

- Draw students' attention to the title of the unit. Read it aloud and ask *What do you love doing?* Elicit answers at random.
- Draw students' attention to the photos. In pairs, have students discuss what they see.

1 Look at the photos. What kind of vacation is it?
Students identify the type of vacation based on photos.

Answer

A cruise

2 Read and identify the activities in the brochure.
Students identify activities based on a text and photos.

Answers

1. cooking, 2. lift weights, 3. go swimming,
4. go climbing, 5. play miniature golf, 6. surfing,
7. snorkeling, 8. get a tan, 9. go shopping,
10. waterskiing

3 Read and underline the correct meanings.
Students choose the correct definitions for vacation activities.

Answers

1. a, 2. a, 3. a, 4. b, 5. b

Extension

Review spelling rules of present participles.

- Elicit the spelling rules for present participles with these deductive grammar prompts:
  » To form the present participle, we add ____ to the base form of the verb. (*-ing*)
  » For most verbs ending in a consonant + vowel + consonant pattern, we ____ the final consonant and then add ____. (double, *-ing*)
  » For verbs ending in a silent *–e*, you ____ the *–e* and then add ____. (drop, *-ing*)
  » For verbs ending in *–ie*, you change the *–ie* to a ____ and then add ____. (*-y, -ing*)
- Have pairs come up with examples for each spelling rule. Encourage students to use verbs from Lessons 1 and 2 when they can. (*doing, cooking, lifting, climbing, snorkeling, waterskiing, surfing, playing, swimming, shopping, getting*)

Wrap-up

Students review vocabulary with a game.

- Students review vacation activities with a game of Pictionary.
- Students form two or three teams. Be sure students understand the rules: They may not use any numbers, symbols or letters. They may not speak. Once a vocabulary word has been pictured, they may not use it again.
- Set a stopwatch for two minutes. A member from each team comes to the board and begins to draw. The other team members try to guess the word. The team member can continue to draw until the stopwatch goes off. Her team gets one point for each picture they guess correctly.
- Then a member from the next team comes up to draw, and the other team members try to guess the activity. The team with the most points at the end wins.

Workbook p. 154, Activity 1

⫸ **Workbook p. 154, Activity 2**

✔ Homework Check!

Workbook p. 154, Activity 1

Answers

1 Look and complete.

1. waterskiing, 2. shopping, 3. tan, 4. climbing,
5. swimming, 6. lifting weights, 7. golf,
8. snorkeling, 9. surfing

Warm-up

Review vocabulary with a game.

- Play charades to review the verbs and verb phrases from the previous lesson.

- Model by acting out one of the verbs, for example, *go climbing*. The student who guesses correctly then comes up and acts out a verb or verb phrase.

- Continue until all verbs or verb phrases have been reviewed or as long as students are engaged.

◄ Complete the e-mail using the correct verbs.

Students complete verb phrases in a passage.

- Draw students' attention to the **Guess What!** box. Read the information aloud and ask students to find examples in the reading: *go swimming, go climbing, play miniature golf, go shopping*.

Answers

top to bottom take, go, play, see, go, going

5 Think Fast! Spell words from the e-mail for a classmate to guess.

Students do a three-minute timed challenge: they look at the pictures and write 10 words of the things they see.

Wrap-up

Students review the verb phrases from the lesson with a game.

- Write the parts of each verb phrase on two separate Post-its: *lift weights, go snorkeling, go waterskiing, go surfing, go climbing, take a class, play miniature golf, go shopping, get a tan, play volleyball*. Have as many Post-its as there are students.

- Stick one Post-it on the back of each student. Don't let students see what's written on their Post-its.

- Have students walk around and ask each other to say what's written on their backs. Provide them with the language if necessary: *Excuse me? Could you tell me what it says on my back?*

- Once students know what word or phrase they have, they must then find the person who has a corresponding word or phrase. For example, the student who has *take* on his Post-it must find the student who has *a class* on hers.

- To make it lively, set a stopwatch for three minutes.

 **Grammar**

Objective

Students will be able to use **likes and dislikes** and *let's* to express preferences and make plans.

Lesson 3   Student's Book p. 114

> ✔ Homework Check!
>
> Workbook p. 154, Activity 2
>
> **Answers**
>
> **2 Read and complete.**
>
> 1. go, 2. snorkeling, 3. cooking, 4. play, 5. play, 6. go

Warm-up

Students categorize activities to review vocabulary and preview the lesson.

- Draw two smiley faces on the board, each at the end of a line to make a scale:

  ☹ ←_____→ ☺

- Elicit the activities from Lesson 2. Model by writing an activity you don't like at one of the scale and one that you like on the other.

- Have students draw a similar scale decide where the activities fall for them.

- In pairs, have students compare and discuss their scales.

 116

1 Look, read and circle the correct option.

Students determine how much people like activities based on pictures.

- Draw students' attention to the *Likes and Dislikes* box. Elicit a few examples.

Answers

Clockwise from the left hate, don't like, like, love, like

2 Write sentences about Jo's family using the clues.

Students write sentences about people's likes and dislikes using cues.

Answers

1. Dad likes fishing. 2. Mom doesn't like fishing.
3. Jo loves camping. 4. Owen hates going to the bathroom in the woods.

3 🎧³⁷ Listen and circle T (True) or F (False).

Students decide if statements are true or false based on a listening.

Answers

1. F (The weather isn't warm.), 2. T, 3. T, 4. F (Everyone likes the idea of going hiking.)

Audio Script

Jo: I love camping! The fresh air, the trees, the lake…! What do you want to do today?

Maggie: Let's go swimming!

Dad: The weather isn't warm today. Can we go fishing?

All, except dad: [groan]

Dad: What do you think, Owen?

Owen: Let's go shopping!

Maggie: Shopping? Where? We're in the woods.

Sara: I know! Let's go hiking. There are a lot of trails around the lake.

Jo: Good idea, Sara.

Maggie: Cool.

[mom and dad mumble in agreement.]

Owen: I like that idea, too. Let's go!

Extension

Play a game of Tic Tac Toe to review gerunds.

- Draw a Tic Tac Toe grid on the board and fill each square with one of the verbs seen in the lesson.

- Have students form two teams, the *X*s and the *O*s and take turns choosing a verb in a square.

- Ask each team to make a sentence using one of the verbs that expresses a like or dislike and the chosen verb.

- If the sentence is correct, place an *X* or *O* in the square. If the sentence is wrong, the square stays in play.

- Continue until one team has three *X*s or *O*s in a row—either horizontally, vertically or diagonally. This team is the winner.

Wrap-up

Students make guesses about who's who in a listening.

- Play the listening again.

- Have students try to identify the Stickman family members in the picture. (From left to right, back: Mom, Dad; front: Owen, Maggie / Sara, Jo.)

- Challenge students to say how they identified each character.

➡ **Workbook p. 155, Activities 1 and 2**

✔ **Homework Check!**

Workbook p. 155, Activities 1 and 2

Answers

1 Look and complete using the correct form of *like, love* or *hate*.

1. loves, 2. hate, 3. don't like, 4. loves,
5. doesn't like

2 Write sentences using the clues.

1. Tom and Katie don't like dancing. 2. My grandparents like surfing the Internet. 3. My brother hates wearing formal clothing. 4. Lizzy loves watching movies. 5. My best friend doesn't like taking selfies.

Warm-up

Practice expressing likes and dislikes with a game.

- Have small groups of three or four brainstorm a list of activities they have covered so far in the unit.

- Play the game Two Truths and a Lie. Model the game by saying three statements expressing your likes and dislikes. One statement should be a lie, for example, *I like fishing. I don't like hiking. I love shopping.* Students try to guess which statement is the lie.

- Students play the game in their groups. When students have finished, have volunteer students say sentences about their classmates' likes and dislikes.

◀ 4 🎧³⁷ **Listen again and mark (✓). What does the Stickman family decide to do?**

Students listen again to identify what the speakers decide to do.

Answer

go hiking

5 **Match the comments and the suggestions.**

Students match statements of likes or dislikes with the suggestion of an activity that makes sense with each statement.

Answers

1. Let's go dancing on Friday. 2. Let's eat some sushi. 3. Let's watch a different one. 4. Let's go shopping. 5. Let's take some classes.

6 **Think Fast! Write five suggestions for the weekend using *Let's*.**

Students do a five-minute timed challenge: they write sentences suggesting weekend activities.

Answers

Answers will vary.

Wrap-up

Students personalize the vocabulary and grammar.

- Have students make cards with some of the activities they like and don't like. They can use the activities from the lessons and others they know.

- Model the activity by saying a sentence to a student using an activity, for example, *I like shopping.* The student then replies with a suggestion, for example, *Let's go to the mall!*

- Have students mingle around the room, making statements and suggestions to each other.

➤ **Workbook pp. 155 and 156, Activities 3 and 4**

117 ◀

Listening & Reading

Objectives

Students will be able to listen for large numbers. They will also be able to identify similarities and differences.

Lesson 5

> ✔ **Homework Check!**
>
> Workbook pp. 155 and 156, Activities 3 and 4
>
> **Answers**
> **3 Read and match.**
> 1. Yes, I do. I love playing FIFA. 2. Yes, she does.
> 3. No, they don't. 4. No, I don't.
> **4 Look and write the suggestions using *Let's*.**
> 1. Let's watch a movie. 2. Let's play volleyball.
> 3. Let's go swimming. 4. Let's listen to music.

Warm-up

Listen to a text about islands for the gist.

- Play the recording for students to listen for general meaning.
- Pairs tell each other what the reading is about. (*islands*)
- Ask *Have you ever been to an island? Do you know any island? What do you know about it?* Have students share their experiences in pairs or small groups.

1 🎧³⁸ **Listen and complete the facts.**

Students listen for specific information to complete a text.

- Draw students' attention to the ***Be Strategic!*** box and read the information aloud.

Answers

1. 8.8, 2. Six hundred million, ten, 3. One hundred and twenty-four million, 4. 7.6

Audio Script

1. There are 8.8 million islands in the world. Most of these islands are uninhabited because they are very small.
2. Six hundred million people live on islands. That's approximately one out of every ten people on Earth!
3. Java is the most populated island. One hundred and twenty-four million people live there. There are also many islands with a small population.
4. Australia is the biggest island! It has 7.6 million square kilometers.

2 🎧³⁹ **Listen and mark (✓). What is on Palmerston Island?**

Students listen for specific information.

Answers

Left to right, top to bottom people, boat, telephone, Internet, school

Audio Script

My name is William and I live with my family on Palmerston Island in the Pacific Ocean. It's part of the Cook Islands—about 3200 kilometers from New Zealand. It's very small and very remote. You need a boat to come to the island. Only 62 people live here. There are two telephones and we only have Internet for four hours a day. There aren't any cars or supermarkets on the island. I go to the Palmerston Lucky School. We don't have a doctor, but we have a very good nurse and a small clinic.

Stop and Think! Critical Thinking

What are the advantages and disadvantages of living on a remote island?

- Ask *Would you like to live on a remote island?*
- Pairs discuss their thoughts on the question. Have them say why. Encourage them to make a pros and cons list.
- Come together as a class and have students share their opinions.

Wrap-up

Students consolidate learning.

- Say *Think about the island described in the listening. What activities do you think you can do there?*
- Students form pairs to discuss the question. Encourage them to use the vocabulary from the unit: *go fishing, go snorkeling, go surfing, go swimming, go waterskiing, get a tan, go hiking*.

➡ **Workbook p. 157, Activity 1**

✔ **Homework Check!**

Workbook p. 157, Activity 1

Answers

1 Read and label the photos.

top to bottom, left to right calf roping, bull riding, rodeo clown

---

Warm-up

Students review and predict information to generate interest.

- Ask *What can you remember about Palmerston Islands?* Ask questions about it and elicit answers from the whole class, for example, *1. How many people live on Palmerston Island? 2. How many telephones are there? 3. Do they have Internet? 4. What don't they have on the islands? 5. What do they have?*

Answers

1. 62, 2, two, 3. Yes, for four hours a day. 4. They don't have cars, supermarkets or a doctor. 5. They have a school, a nurse and a clinic.

- Tell students they are going to read about a boy who lives on one of the islands. Ask *How do you think his life is similar to and different from your life?*
- Brainstorm answers from the whole class.

3 Read and complete the sentences.

Students read a text and complete sentences with information from the text.

Answers

1. friendly, 2. go to school, 3. works, 4. electricity, 5. going surfing and snorkeling

4 Complete the chart. How is life on Palmerston Island similar to / different from life where you live?

Students do a personalization activity: they compare the lifestyle described in the text with life where they live.

Answers

Answers will vary.

Wrap-up

Students have a discussion to consolidate learning and prepare for the next lesson.

- Ask *What do you think the weather's like on Palmerston Island?* Allow students to express their thoughts.
- If possible, have students check the weather of Palmerston Island online. If not possible, show them these graphs:

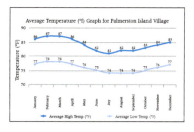

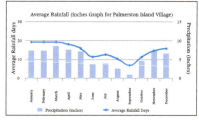

- Ask *How does weather affect the activities you can do?* Pairs discuss.

▸ **Workbook p. 157, Activity 2**

Preparing for the Next Lesson

Ask students to watch an introduction to Russia: goo.gl/Hbb06s or invite them to look around on the website: goo.gl/gQ6RXO.

 *Culture*

Objectives

Students will be able to talk about Russian culture. They will also be able to talk about the importance of traditions.

Lesson 7   Student's Book pp. 118 and 119

> ✔ **Homework Check!**
>
> Workbook p. 157, Activity 2
>
> **Answers**
>
> **2 In your notebook, compare bull riding and calf roping. How are they similar / different?**
> Answers will vary.

Warm-up

Students brainstorm vacation activities they could do in Russia.

- Students form small groups. Draw students' attention to the photos on pages 118 and 119. Tell them to imagine they are doing a podcast about vacation in Russia.

- Ask groups *What activities will you tell your listeners they can do on vacation in Russia?* Elicit an example: *You can go shopping.*

- Groups develop a podcast and share with the class.

1 **How much Russian do you know? Look and label.**
Students identify Russian objects.

 120

Answers

1. troika, 2. balalaika, 3. matryoshka, 4. blini

2 🎧⁴⁰ **Listen and check. Then practice saying the Russian words.**
Students listen to check their answers to Activity 1 and then say words in Russian.

Audio Script

1. This is a troika.
2. This is a balalaika.
3. These are matryoshka dolls.
4. These are blini.

3 🎧⁴¹ **Listen and circle the correct option.**
Students complete the sentences with the correct word based on the listening.

Answers

1. b, 2. a, 3. c, 4. a, 5. a

Audio Script

Some words for typical Russian objects are used in other languages. For example, *matryoshka* dolls are famous all over the world. There are seven dolls of different sizes in each set, one inside the other. In the winter, people often take trips on a *troika*, a sled with three horses. You need hats, coats and scarves to go on a trip on a troika! *Blini* are like pancakes. They're a very popular food in Russia. You can eat it sweet with jam or salty with caviar. Finally, a typical Russian musical instrument is the *balalaika*, a triangle-shaped guitar. People can play solo or in a balalaika orchestra. The balalaika sounds like this.

Wrap-up

Students compare their culture(s) with Russian culture.

- Tell students to think about their culture(s). Ask *Can you think of any similar musical instruments that are in your culture? What about transportation? Food? Folk art?*

- Have students discuss their answers in pairs.

➠ **(No homework today.)**

Warm-up

Students review Russian words with a game.

- Play a game of Hangman to review words from the listening in Lesson 7.

- Choose one of the words and draw a blank for each letter, for example, *caviar*: __ __ __ __ __ __.

- Elicit a letter from your students. If they say a letter that is in the word, write it in the blank.

- If the letter is not in the word, begin to draw a stick figure, starting with a circle for the head. For each letter that is called not in the word, draw another part of the stick figure's body.

- Continue until a student guesses *caviar* or the body is complete.

- Repeat the procedure with other words seen in the lesson.

4 Look and underline. What is the topic of the text?
Students predict what a text will be about.

Answer

b

5 Read and underline the parts you find interesting.
Students read the text and identify things in the article that interest them.

Answers

Answers will vary.

6 Find and underline these items in the text.
Students read to find specific information.

Answers

1. cold, snow, -25° Celsius, 2. eleven time zones,
3. Anadyr, 4. *Ded Moroz, Sneguroshka*, 5. *Epiphany*

Extension

Students do research on time zones.

- Tell students to do some research on time zones by answering these questions: *What is your country's time zone? Is there more than one time zone? How are time zones determined?*

- Have students present their findings in small groups.

Stop and Think! Value

Do you like observing traditions? What is your favorite tradition?

- Tell students to name some Russian traditions they learned about from the reading.

- Have students say some of their national traditions and which ones they celebrate.

- Have pairs meet to answer the questions: *Do you like observing traditions? What is your favorite tradition?*

Wrap-up

Students compare two places.

- Have students think about the activities you can do on Palmerston Island and in Siberia. Ask *Which place would you rather go on vacation? Why?*

- Pairs discuss the questions.

➠ **(No homework today.)**

Teaching Tip

Teaching Reading Techniques

Reading is an important part of learning English. Tell your students to think about how they read in their own language. For example, tell them to think about how they read a newspaper. They might skim a newspaper, looking for the main ideas. They read the headlines, the captions, the first and last paragraphs or sentences of articles to get the gist of what's there. They might scan the newspaper, looking for important, or key, words, facts or phrases to find specific information. Point out that they do not always have to understand every word to understand the text.

 **Project**

Objective
Students will be able to make a Free Time Activities Survey.

Lesson 9   Student's Book p. 120

Warm-up
Students categorize activities.
- Have students brainstorm vacation activities covered in the unit; for instance: *going swimming, going climbing, playing miniature golf, going shopping, getting a tan*, etc.
- Have pairs categorize the activities into two groups, *Indoor Activities* and *Outdoor Activities*. Encourage students to add other activities they know.

1 Read and mark (✓) activities you love doing.
Students mark indoor and outdoor activities they like doing.

Answer
Answers will vary.

2 🎧⁴² Listen and complete the missing information.
Students complete survey forms with information from the listening.

Answers
Sam, top to bottom Sam Smith, going swimming and playing volleyball, watching movies
Donna, top to bottom London, playing volleyball, playing miniature golf

---

Audio Script
PRESENTER: Hi. Welcome Donna, Nat, Sam, Simon and Sue. Thank you for agreeing to participate in our survey.
PRESENTER: You probably don't have much free time, but I am sure there are activities you love doing when you do have a chance. And there are some activities that you don't like. Here is the list of activities we are interested in. Who wants to begin?
SAM: I do.
PRESENTER: Very well. What's your name?
SAM: Sam Smith.
PRESENTER: Where are you from?
SAM: Miami.
PRESENTER: What do you do?
SAM: I'm a student.
PRESENTER: Which activities do you love?
SAM: I love going swimming and playing volleyball!
PRESENTER: Which ones do you dislike?
SAM: Hmm, I don't like watching movies.
PRESENTER: And which ones do you hate?
SAM: I hate eating out at fancy restaurants. It's too expensive!
PRESENTER: Thank you, Sam. What about you, Donna?
DONNA: My name is Donna Blues.

PRESENTER: Where are you from?
DONNA: I'm from London.
PRESENTER: How old are you?
DONNA: I am 14 years old.
PRESENTER: What do you do?
DONNA: I am also a student.
PRESENTER: Which activities do you love?
DONNA: I love taking classes. I'm taking pizza-making classes now. And I love reading, too.
PRESENTER: Which ones do you dislike?
DONNA: I don't like playing volleyball.
PRESENTER: And which ones do you hate?
DONNA: I hate playing miniature golf. I'm terrible at it!
PRESENTER: Thank you, Donna. Who would like to go next?

---

3 🎧⁴² Listen again and complete the questions.
Students listen again and complete the survey questions with words from the audio.

Answers
1. your name, 2. are you from, 3. do you do, 4. do you love, 5. do you dislike, 6. ones do you hate

Wrap-up
Students ask each other survey questions.
- Pairs ask and answer the questions in the surveys.

Warm-up

Students think of icons or images to use with
their surveys.

- Draw students' attention to the poster on page
  121, specifically the pictures above each graph. Tell
  them to tell you what they represent. Refer them
  to the list in Activity 1 on page 120 if necessary.
  (*cooking, reading, watching movies, eating out, swimming,
  playing volleyball, fishing, playing mini golf*)

- Have students take out their lists of vacation
  activities from the Warm-up in Lesson 9.

- Pairs think about icons or images they might use to
  represent the activities.

◀ **Make a survey about vacation activities.**

Students follow steps to create a survey. They survey
five people about vacation activities and present the
results of their surveys.

> ### The Digital Touch
> To incorporate digital media in the project, suggest
> one or more of the following:
> - Have students make a PowerPoint or Google
>   Slides presentation of their survey.
> - Build a survey online:
>   https://freeonlinesurveys.com/#/.
> Note that students should have the option to do a
> task on paper or digitally.

Wrap-up

Students display their surveys.

- Display students' surveys in your classroom.

- Have students share the information in their
  surveys with their classmates.

▶ **Workbook p. 156, Activities 1–3 (Review)**

 **Review**

Objective

Students will be able to consolidate their understanding of the vocabulary and grammar learned in the unit.

Lesson 11   Student's Book p. 122

> ✔ **Homework Check!**
>
> Workbook p. 156, Activities 1–3 (Review)
>
> **Answers**
> **1 Look and circle the correct option.**
> 1. go, 2. play, 3. play, 4. go, 5. play
> **2 Complete the dialogues using the correct forms of the verbs.**
> 1. playing, doesn't, 2. doing, cooking, 3. reading, to read, go
> **3 Answers the questions in your notebook.**
> Answers will vary.

Warm-up

Students list the vocabulary and grammar they have learned in the unit.

- Tell students to think of what they've learned in this unit.
- Elicit and list the grammar and vocabulary on the board. Vocabulary: vacation activities: *climbing, cooking, get a tan, lift weights, miniature golf, shopping, snorkeling, surfing, swimming, waterskiing*. Grammar: likes and dislikes (*love, like, don't / doesn't like, hate* + gerund); *let's*.

 124

1 Read and match.

Students match vacation activities with icons.

Answers

top to bottom, left to right 2, 5, 9, 3, 4, 1, 8, 7, 6, 7, 10

2 Make a list. Which activities do you do in water?

Students identify the vacation activities done in water.

Answers

go snorkeling, go surfing, go swimming, go waterskiing

3 Read and solve the puzzle.

Students use clues to complete a crossword puzzle with vacation activities.

Answers

1. cook, 2. weights, 3. play, 4. tan, 5. water, 6. climbing, 7. shopping

Wrap-up

Students review vocabulary with a game.

- Have students review vacation activities with a game of Taboo.
- Have students form two teams. They turn their seats so their backs are to the board. In front of each team, facing the board, is a "hot seat."
- Write a vacation activity on the board.
- One member from each team sits in the hot seat. These students can see the vacation activity, but the other students cannot.
- Set a stopwatch for one minute. Once you say, *Go!* the teams have one minute, using only verbal clues, to describe the vacation activity written on the board. The only rule, or taboo, is that the student cannot say the word on the board.
- The round is over when the stopwatch goes off or a student says the correct word. That student wins a point for his team.
- The team with the most points at the end wins.

➡ **(No homework today.)**

Warm-up

Students remember what they reviewed in the previous lesson.

- Ask students to say what they've reviewed. Elicit *vacation activities*.
- Ask students to say what they will be reviewing today. Elicit *likes and dislikes*, and *let's*.

◄ Look and complete the sentences. Then number the photos.

Students complete sentences with the correct verbs and match each sentence to a photo.

Answers

1. doing, 2. reading, 3. listening, 4. playing; *left to right* 2, 4, 3, 1

5 Read and number the lines of the dialogue.

Students put a dialogue in order.

Answers

top to bottom, left to right 5, 7, 3, 1, 4, 6, 2

? Big Question

Students are given the opportunity to revisit the Big Question and reflect on it.

- Ask students to turn to the unit opener on page 111 and think about the question "What do you love doing?"
- Ask students to think about the discussions they've had about activities, the readings and recordings and the surveys they made.
- Students form small groups to discuss the following:
  » How often do you go on vacation?
  » Do you prefer active vacations, doing lots of outdoor activities or more relaxing vacations? Why?
  » How important is it to do what you love?

★ Scorecard

Hand out (and/or project) a *Scorecard*. Have students fill in their *Scorecards* for this unit.

 Study for the unit test.

Verb List

Base Form	Present Simple: 3rd Person Singular	Verb + –ing
be	is[1]	being
brush	brushes[2]	brushing
call	calls	calling
check	checks	checking
circle	circles	circling[4]
climb	climbs	climbing
compose	composes	composing[4]
cook	cooks	cooking
dance	dances	dancing[4]
delete	deletes	deleting[4]
do	does[2]	doing
eat	eats	eating
e-mail	e-mails	e-mailing
exercise	exercises	exercising[4]
get	gets	getting[5]
go	goes[2]	going
have	has[1]	having[4]
jump	jumps	jumping
lift	lifts	lifting
listen to	listens to	listening to
live	lives	living[4]
look	looks	looking
make	makes	making[4]
open	opens	opening
play	plays	playing
print	prints	printing
read	reads	reading
relax	relaxes[2]	relaxing
reply	replies[3]	replying
save	saves	saving[4]
send	sends	sending
share	shares	sharing[4]
shop	shops	shopping[5]
sit	sits	sitting[5]
sleep	sleeps	sleeping
study	studies[3]	studying
surf	surfs	surfing
swim	swims	swimming[5]
take	takes	taking[4]
text	texts	texting
use	uses	using[4]
wake up	wakes up	waking[4] up
watch	watches[2]	watching
wear	wears	wearing
write	writes	writing[4]

[1] These are irregular verbs.   [2]Add –es with third person singular.
[3]The –y becomes –ies with third person singular.   [4]The –e is removed in verb + –ing.
[5]The consonant doubles in verb + –ing.